Land Marks

New site proposals by twenty-two original pioneers of environmental art

Cecile Abish Alice Aycock Agnes Denes
Harriet Feigenbaum Jackie Ferrara
Richard Fleischner Helen and Newton Harrison
Nancy Holt Ana Mendieta Mary Miss
Robert Morris Dennis Oppenheim Beatrice Perry
Jody Pinto Charles Ross Michael Singer
Alan Sonfist Robert Stackhouse
Michelle Stuart Athena Tacha Carolee Thea

Exhibition Curator: Linda Weintraub
September 16 — October 28, 1984 Edith C. Blum Art Institute
Bard College Center Annandale-on-Hudson, New York

This exhibition is sponsored by grants from the Edith C. Blum Foundation, the National Endowment for the Arts, and the New York State Council on the Arts.

This exhibition was organized and circulated by the Edith C. Blum Art Institute,
Milton and Sally Avery Center for the Arts,
Bard College Center, Annandale-on-Hudson, New York, 1984.

Catalogue design: Dick Higgins
Photography: Ralph Gabriner, Jerry Smith, Steven Houghton
Typography: Bauer Typography
Manufactured in the United States of America.

Library of Congress Catalogue Card Number 84-071424

ISBN 0-941276-04-X

Edition: 2500 copies

Table of Contents

5 Curator's Introduction

Artists' Entries

8 Cecile Abish
10 Ana Mendieta
12 Harriet Feigenbaum
14 Agnes Denes
16 Carolee Thea
18 Mary Miss
19 Dennis Oppenheim
22 Alice Aycock
24 Beatrice Perry
26 Helen and Newton Harrison
28 Charles Ross
30 Jackie Ferrara
32 Michael Singer
34 Jody Pinto
36 Alan Sonfist
38 Richard Fleischner
40 Robert Stackhouse
42 Nancy Holt
44 Michelle Stuart
46 Robert Morris
48 Athena Tacha

Catalogue Essays

57 Lawrence Alloway
61 Erik Kiviat
67 Shelley Rice
77 Daniel Simberloff

87 Artists' Biographies

1

2

3

4

5

6

7

8

9

10

11

12

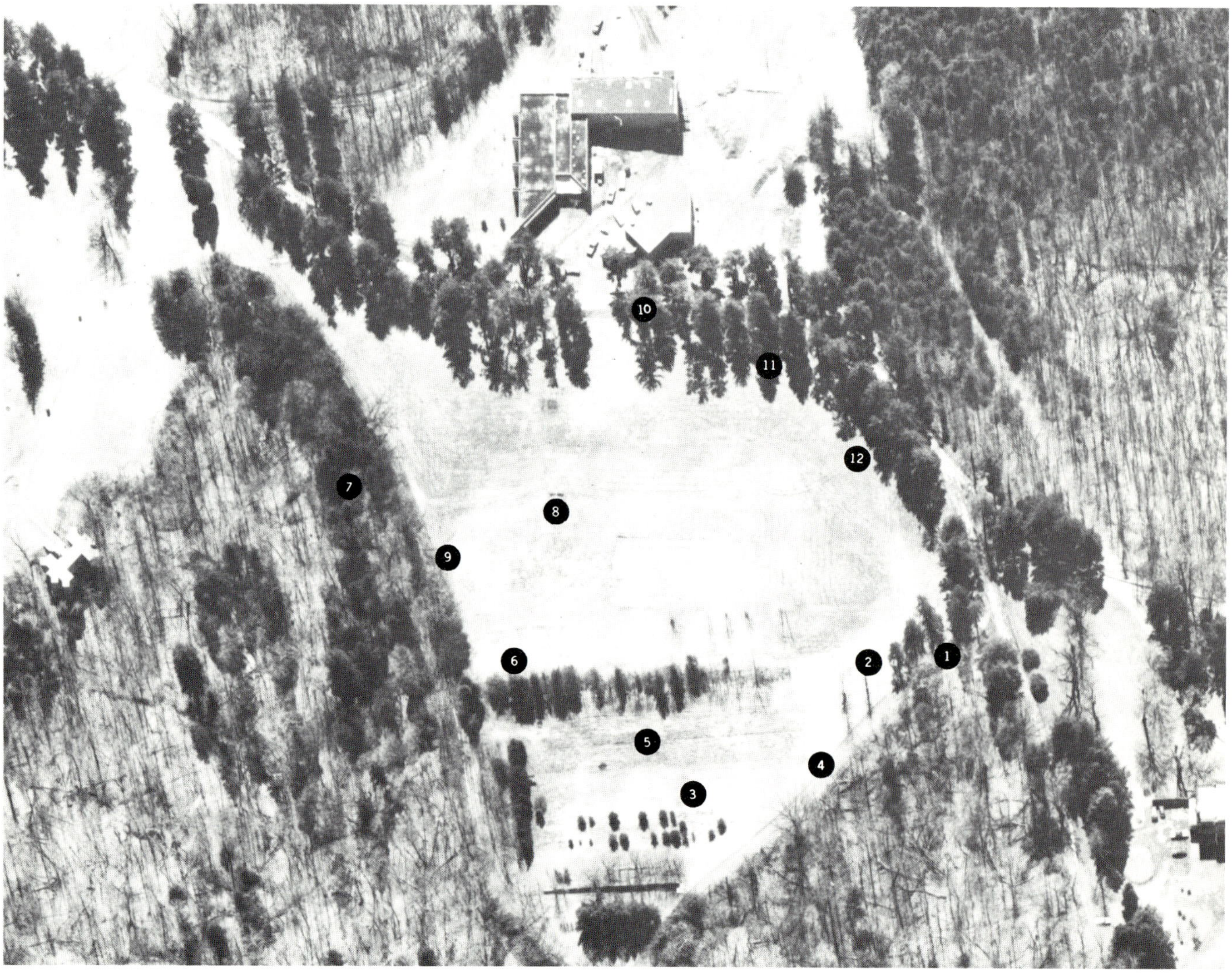

Curator's Introduction

Throughout the vicissitudes of history, artists have variously celebrated the beauties and decried the horrors of the world. They have retreated into fantasy as often as they have engaged in polemics, and they have presented in cogent form the fears and dangers that surrounded them. Artists have served as guardians of tradition, but they have also revolutionized expectations and proclaimed whole eras obsolete.

In organizing this exhibition, twenty-two artists were invited to make these aspects of contemporary art explicit. They were offered a commission to design a work of art for the identical outdoor site. The show is based on the premise that all site-related sculpture carries meaning, a factor that emerges from the coalition of three elements: one, the sculpture is conceived by man or woman; two, it takes material form; and three, it is set in the natural environment. As a result, it is in itself, a product of the relationship among humans, technology, and nature.

Works either favor the rigid, standardized and geometric forms of the urban environment or the fluid, unpredictable character of the natural environment. Continuity between art and the land implies harmony between humans and nature. Discrete and obtrusive forms on the other hand, reveal a literal attempt to separate humans from nature. In an era when the balance between these three elements is so precarious, it seems prudent to seek guidance among those who, along with politicians, philosophers, and writers, have traditionally assumed the role of spokesperson for society—the artists.

Although several decades have passed since sculpture first burst beyond the confines of the gallery and museum space, no systematic and comprehensive examination of current American sculpture designed for rural outdoor settings has been undertaken. This project is structured in order to review this aspect of contemporary art among the generation of artists who made a commitment to it at least fifteen years ago. Because all artists are responding to a common problem, the exhibition encourages a search for commonalities and an exploration of differences among their works. Finally, it directs critical attention toward a sphere of artistic activity that has been neglected by critics, journalists, and scholars despite the fact that the exploration of environmental issues has been sustained by this generation of artists.

The four scholars who were invited to consider these issues in this catalogue offer four distinct sets of qualifications. Their essays reveal the uniqueness of each approach and provide the reader with information that derives from the great expanse of knowledge that they represent compositely.

Lawrence Alloway, whose first book, *Venice Biennale: 1895-1968* (1968), and whose most recent book, *Network: Art in the Complex Present* (1984), bracket a long and distinguished career as a professor of art history (at Bennington College and at the State University of New York at Stony Brook), as a curator (at the Solomon R. Guggenheim Museum), and as a critic (at the *Nation* and *Artforum*). An independent thinker who has disassociated himself from schools of criticism, his career has spanned both decades and movements. His other books include *Violent America: The Movies 1946-1964* (1971), *American Pop Art* (1974), and *Topics in American Art Since 1945* (1975).

Shelley Rice, currently a member of the faculty of New York University and at the School of Visual Arts. Rice has trained as an art historian with emphasis on 20th-century photography. Since 1978, she has broadened her area of interest to encompass installations, artists' books, and video. Her articles have appeared in *Art in America, The New Republic, Art Journal, Afterimage,* and *Picture,* and she has been Photography Criticism Editor for *The Village Voice.* Rice has been awarded a Danforth Foundation Graduate Fellowship, a New York State Council on the Arts Video Writing Fellowship, and two National Endowment for the Arts grants. She has written columns for *The Village Voice, Soho Weekly News,* and *Artforum.*

Erik Kiviat, Research Associate in Ecology at Bard College where he taught for eight years and was director of the Field Station. He has twenty years of experience in the natural history of the Hudson Valley, specializing in the conservation of rare species and communities. He is currently a member of the Board of Directors of Hudsonia, a non-profit research institute, and he has published forty articles in technical and popular journals. Kiviat's qualifications to discuss the work in this exhibition extend beyond his intimate knowledge of the site. For ten years he was a poet and a visual artist. His dissertation topic combines these interests. In it he is exploring the relationship between wetlands and all aspects of human society, including culture and art.

Daniel Simberloff, internationally recognized ecologist, who has expanded his sphere of academic interest to include the implications of biology for the visual arts, e.g. the influence of neurobiology and sociobiology on aesthetic considerations in art. He has also published essays relating these theories to bluegrass music and the novels of Thomas Pynchon, and has conducted extensive research on familial organization in Saylorsburg.

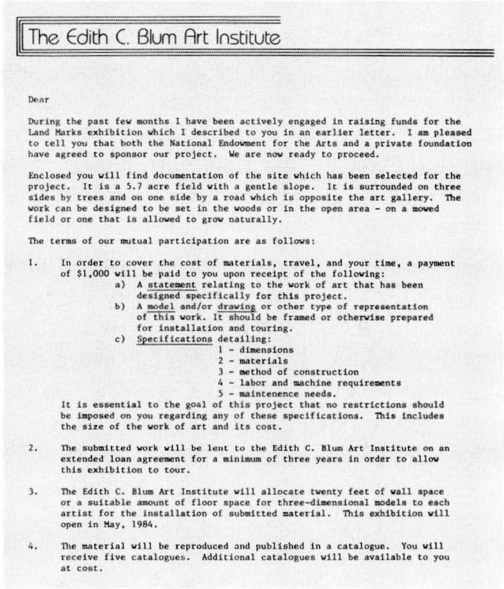

The Edith C. Blum Art Institute

Dear

During the past few months I have been actively engaged in raising funds for the Land Marks exhibition which I described to you in an earlier letter. I am pleased to tell you that both the National Endowment for the Arts and a private foundation have agreed to sponsor our project. We are now ready to proceed.

Enclosed you will find documentation of the site which has been selected for the project. It is a 5.7 acre field with a gentle slope. It is surrounded on three sides by trees and on one side by a road which is opposite the art gallery. The work can be designed to be set in the woods or in the open area - on a mowed field or one that is allowed to grow naturally.

The terms of our mutual participation are as follows:

1. In order to cover the cost of materials, travel, and your time, a payment of $1,000 will be paid to you upon receipt of the following:
   a) A statement relating to the work of art that has been designed specifically for this project.
   b) A model and/or drawing or other type of representation of this work. It should be framed or otherwise prepared for installation and touring.
   c) Specifications detailing:
      1 - dimensions
      2 - materials
      3 - method of construction
      4 - labor and machine requirements
      5 - maintenence needs.

   It is essential to the goal of this project that no restrictions should be imposed on you regarding any of these specifications. This includes the size of the work of art and its cost.

2. The submitted work will be lent to the Edith C. Blum Art Institute on an extended loan agreement for a minimum of three years in order to allow this exhibition to tour.

3. The Edith C. Blum Art Institute will allocate twenty feet of wall space or a suitable amount of floor space for three-dimensional models to each artist for the installation of submitted material. This exhibition will open in May, 1984.

4. The material will be reproduced and published in a catalogue. You will receive five catalogues. Additional catalogues will be available to you at cost.

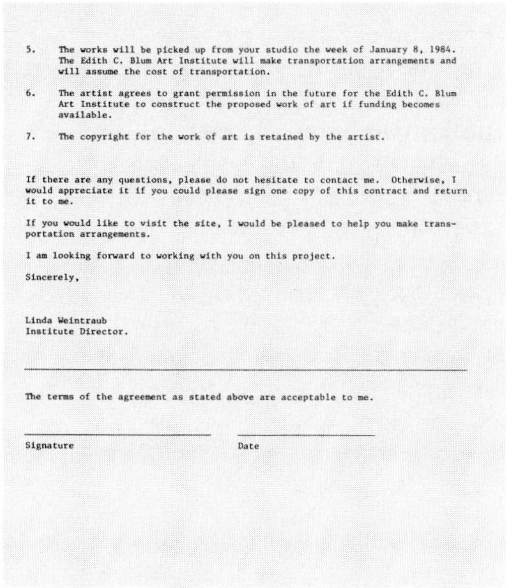

5. The works will be picked up from your studio the week of January 8, 1984. The Edith C. Blum Art Institute will make transportation arrangements and will assume the cost of transportation.

6. The artist agrees to grant permission in the future for the Edith C. Blum Art Institute to construct the proposed work of art if funding becomes available.

7. The copyright for the work of art is retained by the artist.

If there are any questions, please do not hesitate to contact me. Otherwise, I would appreciate it if you could please sign one copy of this contract and return it to me.

If you would like to visit the site, I would be pleased to help you make transportation arrangements.

I am looking forward to working with you on this project.

Sincerely,

Linda Weintraub
Institute Director.

The terms of the agreement as stated above are acceptable to me.

Signature　　　　Date

Simberloff is a Professor in the Department of Biological Studies at Florida State University. Since 1968 he has been an invited lecturer at over 100 conferences worldwide, an editor on five scientific journals, and has published 73 technical papers.

In order to initiate this project, the participating artists were sent information detailing a single site for which they were invited to design a work of art. They received photographs, topographical maps, soil analysis, vegetation descriptions, information on frost levels, rainfall, and underground cables. They were informed that this project was fashioned to encourage the fullest expression of their artistic intentions. Neither practical nor financial limitations were being imposed. They were free to indulge in the truest representation of their creative wills.

The site was selected because it contained no peculiar nor dramatic characteristics. It provided the artists with as neutral a terrain as possible. This assured that the works of art would be easily understood by those who could not visit the site. Furthermore, the scale of the site permitted the artist either to submit to or to dominate the natural setting.

Another benefit is the varied character of the site. Artists could select among three distinct types of geographical situations. One six-acre area is circumscribed by a 2000-foot long horseshoe path. This field is tended and mowed. It undulates gently and rises at one distinct location off center. There is also a smaller field that is left untended and is less visible to visitors. Wild flowers, small trees, berries, and tall grasses grow in profusion in this area. The two fields are separated by a row of trees. On the opposite side of the path is a wooded ravine. Trees are tall; most are deciduous. In summer the undergrowth is so dense that the area becomes inpenetrable.

This site, therefore, provides artists with distinct choices and varied possibilities. No restrictions were imposed; the artists were free to select the entire area or an element of it. They were given the option of recontouring the land, piping in water, mowing the unmowed area or stipulating that the tended area remain uncultivated. Their choices provide clues to the mode in which the artist related to the site.

The first section of this catalogue contains reproductions of the artists' submitted proposals. Each proposal consists of a visual presentation and a statement. As a unit, this body of work presented a challenge to the scholars who contributed the essays that follow in the second section of the catalogue. The four scholars grouped the thematic and formal decisions represented in these works of art according to their particular concerns. Their essays present a penetrating analysis of the relationship between this assemblage of work and its antecedents, as well as carefully considered speculation into the philosophic and sociological implications of the work.

The significance of this project for the visitor to the gallery, or the reader of this catalogue, can only be derived by undertaking a comparable examination of the works of art. The following variables provide insight into the manner in which twenty-two of America's foremost artists balance the human, the natural, and the technological elements of the contemporary world:

—**Responsiveness to environmental changes:** light, season, moisture, temperature.

—**Choice of materials:** precious or common, industrial or natural.

—**Sources of imagery:** ancient archeological ruins, industrial complexes, domestic architecture, formal gardens, farm structures, etc.

—**Durability:** extended life span or brief duration, inert or evolving.

—**Scale:** heroic or modest.
—**Structural orientation:** aligned with the horizon, protruding from the earth, nestled into the terrain.
—**Construction techniques:** manual labor, industrial machinery, advanced technology.
—**Utility:** nonfunctional or employed for skating, performing, meditating, walking, etc.
—**Time:** reference to astronomical, geological, botanical, mythological, or conceptual time.
—**Documentation:** projects are exhibited as blueprints, xeroxes, videos, models, miniatures, renderings, drawings.
—**Visual orientation:** attention focused upward/downward, inward/outward, near/far.
—**Metaphor:** meaning may be veiled or explicit, specific or general.

It becomes evident, once this analysis has been undertaken, that the energy that propelled the initial experiments in the outdoor arena has been sustained into the 1980s. Artists have continued to probe the potential of this kind of activity. They have persisted because it remains fertile territory for exploration.

Beyond the vitality that has been demonstrated among the individual artists, however, is the impact of work when viewed as an aggregate. Individual artists seem to have progressed in parallel fashion, endowing the movement with the vigor of shared innovation.

The enormous variety among the submitted proposals is explored in the essays that follow. But there is also a consistency of transformation that is remarkable. No convenient network of information has existed to unify the group. Most works have been located away from the metropolitan centers where they are inaccessible to the artists and where they receive scant media attention.

Shared characteristics emerging from hermetic activity endow these changes with special significance. They become most meaningful when compared to the tenor of work that was created in the 60s and early 70s. It was at this time that artists found the confined space and the inert environment of the museum incompatible with their artistic needs. They left the museum in pursuit of nature's perpetual transformations, its interlocking and interdependent systems, its vastness, and its unpredictability.

Their response to these aspects of the great outdoors imposed on the art of this era all its most controversial elements. These are the very elements that have been eliminated in the site work of the 1980s. For instance, none of the works proposed in the **Land Marks** exhibition are designed to self-destruct. The artists no longer reject the idea of art assuming an end state or a finished form, and they are not neglectful of the visual appeal of fine materials and meticulous design. In fact, they all present a handsome and imposing presence in the landscape. The original involvement with process, network and system that evolved from Minimal and Conceptual art has been substituted with practical designs for architectural structures. Furthermore, they are no longer content to locate the work in remote settings where the audience contact is dependent on media surrogates. Instead, and overwhelmingly, the attention has been directed toward the direct physical and psychological involvement of the viewer.

In the first flush of excitement, environmental art inhabited the polar extremes of possibility. The work either acquiesced to the forces of nature or was conceived in the spirit of defiance. Contemporary projects no longer pluck the heads off daisies, set a reflective surface in the landscape, or disappear into conceptual oblivion. Neither do they presume to manipulate whole continents and the constellations that spread across the skies. The current projects have discovered something unique within this context—they are based on human scale. They address human needs and are designed to facilitate human experience.

The newest site works offer the viewer an insight of lasting consequence. They assert that the cultural and artistic output of society is as much a part of the ecology of the earth as any geological formation, or any biological organism. Perhaps they are suggesting that the human race need not submit to the whims of nature, nor must it attempt to dominate and tame the forces of nature. A new homeostasis has been discovered.

This project has been made possible through the aid of generous grants from:

The Edith C. Blum Foundation
The National Endowment for the Arts
The New York State Council on the Arts

The Edith C. Blum Art Institute is grateful to the following individuals for the numerous and varied contributions they made to this effort:

The Artists—Cecile Abish, Alice Aycock, Agnes Denes, Harriet Feigenbaum, Jackie Ferrara, Richard Fleischner, Helen and Newton Harrison, Nancy Holt, Ana Mendieta, Mary Miss, Robert Morris, Dennis Oppenheim, Beatrice Perry, Jody Pinto, Charles Ross, Michael Singer, Alan Sonfist, Robert Stackhouse, Michelle Stuart, Athena Tacha, and Carolee Thea.

The Scholars—Lawrence Alloway, Shelley Rice, Erik Kiviat, and Daniel Simberloff.

The Advisors—Wilbur Friedman, Eric Siegeltuch, and Richard Griffiths.

The Bard College Staff—Dimitri Papadimitriou, Donise English, Lucy Ferriss, Tina Iraca Green, Mirko Gabler, and Judy Samoff.

Linda Weintraub
Institute Director

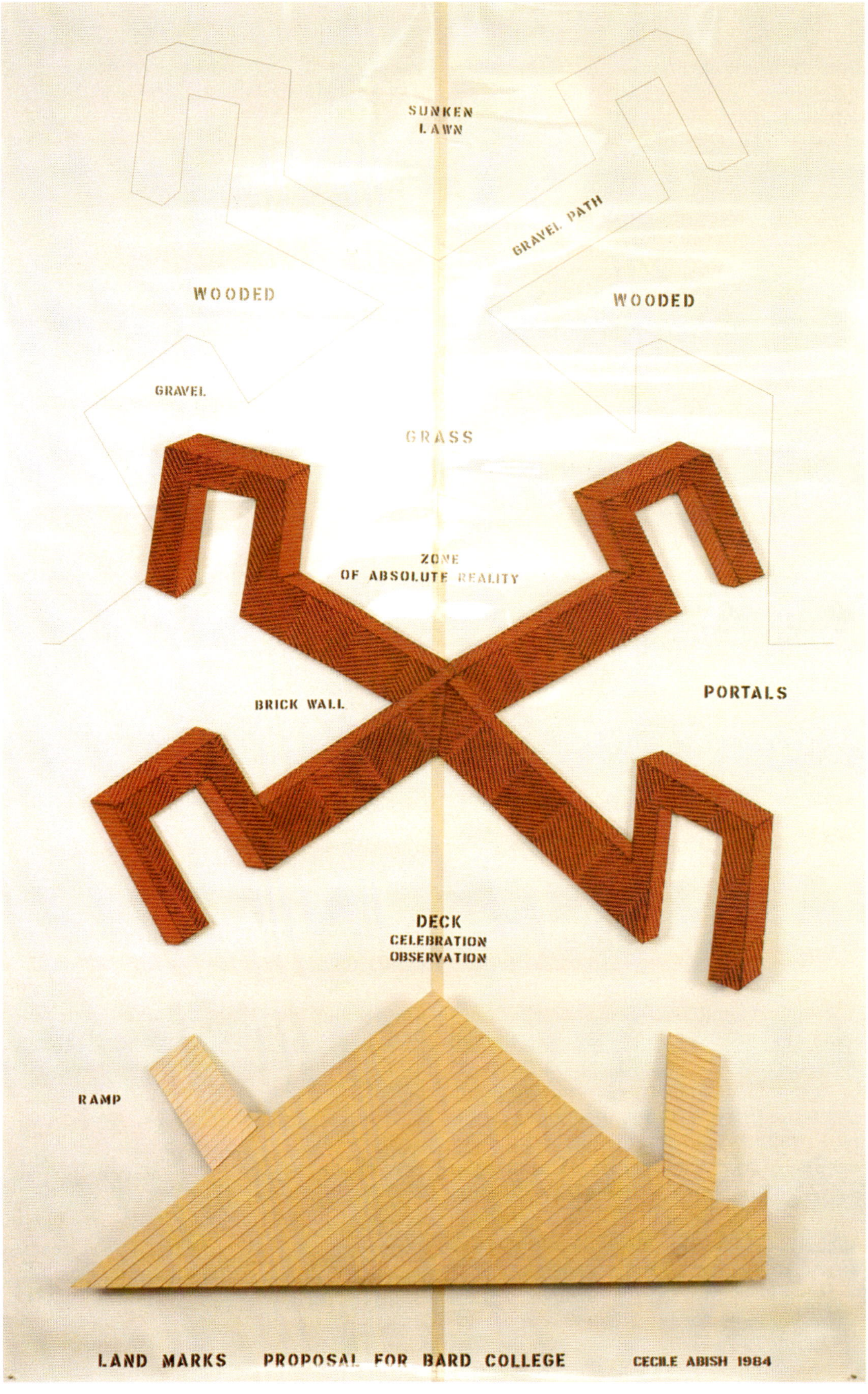

1A.

1) CECILE ABISH

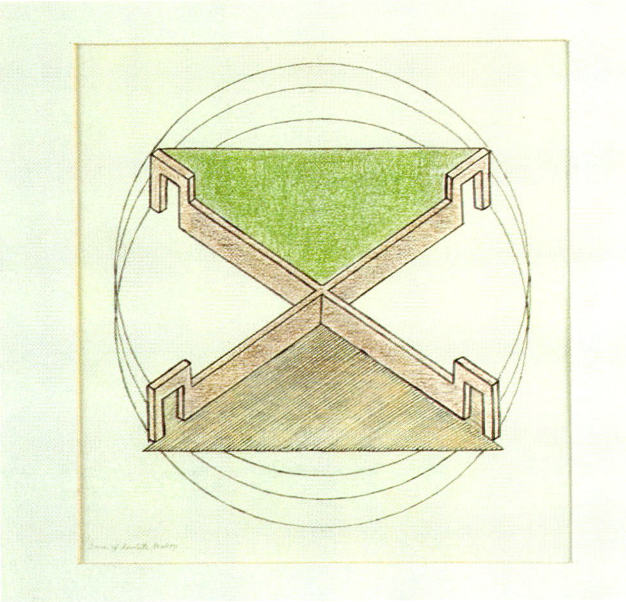

1B.

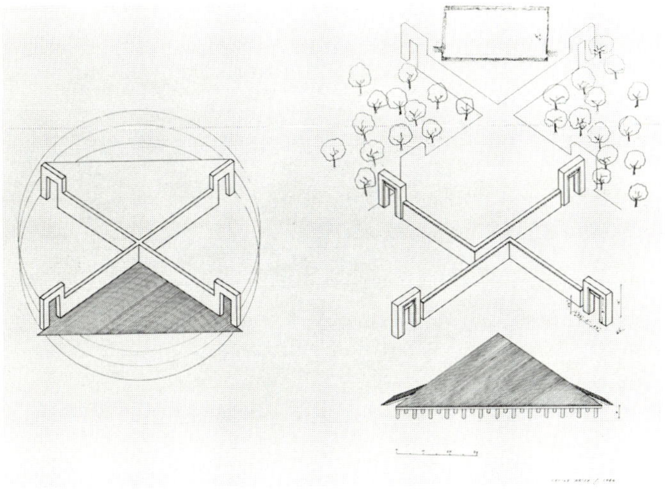

1C.

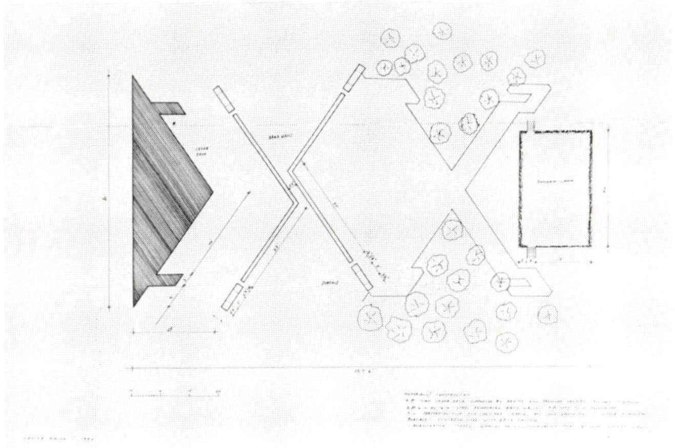

1D.

Artist's statement

What they say when they say, enter
is that death is a door
Don't you believe it

What they say when they say, leave
Is that you don't step in
the same stream twice
They just can't conceive
of sliding doors.
October 29, 1982

Epicurean arrangements[1] was conceived as an invitation to play, an invitation for events to unfold and in repeating themselves to initiate an archetype. In that respect the interrelated elements: Extended L shaped brick walls, narrow passage

(statement continues, p. 51)

1A. Wall piece—wood, rubber, paper, wax, ink, 8′6″ × 5′8″ × 2″
1B. Drawing—graphite, ink, oil, wax crayon on paper, 24 × 32″
1C. Drawing—graphite, ink, oil, wax crayon on paper, 24 × 32″
1D. Drawing—graphite, ink, oil, wax crayon on paper, 24 × 32″
Lent courtesy the artist

EPICUREAN ARRANGEMENTS

2) ANA MENDIETA

Artist's statement. During the past 10 years my work, as a dialogue between nature and the mythical female body, has evolved dialectically in response to diverse landscapes as an emotional, sexual, biological affirmation of being.

Opposed to the Earthworks of the 1970s, which use nature in its most literal sense, my purpose and interest is rooted in nature's symbolical meaning. My works do not belong to the modernist tradition, which exploits physical properties and an enlarged scale of materials. Nor is it akin to the commercially historical-self-conscious assertions of what is called post-modernism.

My art is grounded on the primordial accumulations, the unconscious urges that animate the world, not in an attempt to redeem the past, but rather in confrontation with the void, the orphanhood, the unbaptized earth of the beginning, the time that from within the earth looks upon us.

Because I have never made "paper art" and am used to working directly on location in the simplest and most direct way, my method of construction would be as follows:

First, to draw directly with the earth the image on the chosen site (9 feet × 5 feet), and to build the spirals to the desired height and width (4 inches × 10 inches).

Second, to cover the earth-drawing with Phillips 66 plastic erosion membrane in order to ensure the protection of the piece.

Third, to plant the seedlings of an English grass called RACROSTES, known for its close cropping growth and fine texture, which helps eliminate sedimentation of the earth and which makes upkeep of the piece easier.

Needless to say, proper irrigation will be crucial to the welfare of the work. Hand-trimming will be the only way to maintain it.

The work for Bard is meant by its materials and scale to utilize the subtlety and delicacy of nature.

4 line-grass-spirals composing a figure to be realized at the *#8 slide site* facing. The figure is 9′ × 5′. Each line of the spiral is 10 inches (at its width) × 4 inches in elevation.

Budget

Top soil	$ 500.00
Phillips 66 plastic membrane	2000.00
Racrostes grass seeds	500.00
Total	$3000.00

Equipment

Truck to transport top soil to site, small garden tools.

2. Graphite on paper, 102 × 56½″
Lent courtesy the artist

LA MAJA DE YERBA 1984

Artist's statement. The proposal incorporates the open 5.7 acre field and the adjacent ravine abutting it to the southeast. The open field is to be terraced upward in an eccentric spiral derived from the contours of the surrounding terrain. The terraces will slope down from the outer edges inward (less than 1%) to control and catch water run-off. The water (essentially rain water) will be directed into a network of stepped canals running diagonally across the terraces from east to west. Simply put, the water will run downhill in a pyramidal spiral along the inside walls of the terraces until it comes to a canal opening. This action will result in gently flowing waterfalls increasing to rapids, echoing the falls and rapids that flow into the Hudson and related to a specific woodland site on campus.

The water flowing westward will end in a drainage system near the Norway Spruces along the roadway. The eastward flow will cascade down into a terraced ravine. The cascade will terminate in a shallow (depth controlled) lake that echoes the natural contours of the land. In winter this lake will freeze and become a skating rink. This section of the ravine containing the skating rink would be protected by 10-16′ stone faced cliffs. Indoor recreation facilities should be built into the cliff face (a place to have a cup of coffee and put on skates etc. with windows facing the rink). The intended result is for a dramatically landscaped and thoroughly useable park. Arrangements of huge pines in strategic and esthetic patterns would serve as additional windbreaks for the rink and the entire terraced ravine. Changing views of the water patterns and trees are an important aspect of the design. A slow walk up the spiral terraces is intended to provide a variety of perspective views of the row of White Pines and Norway Spruces along the road-

(statement continues, p. 51)

(detail)

3) HARRIET FEIGENBAUM

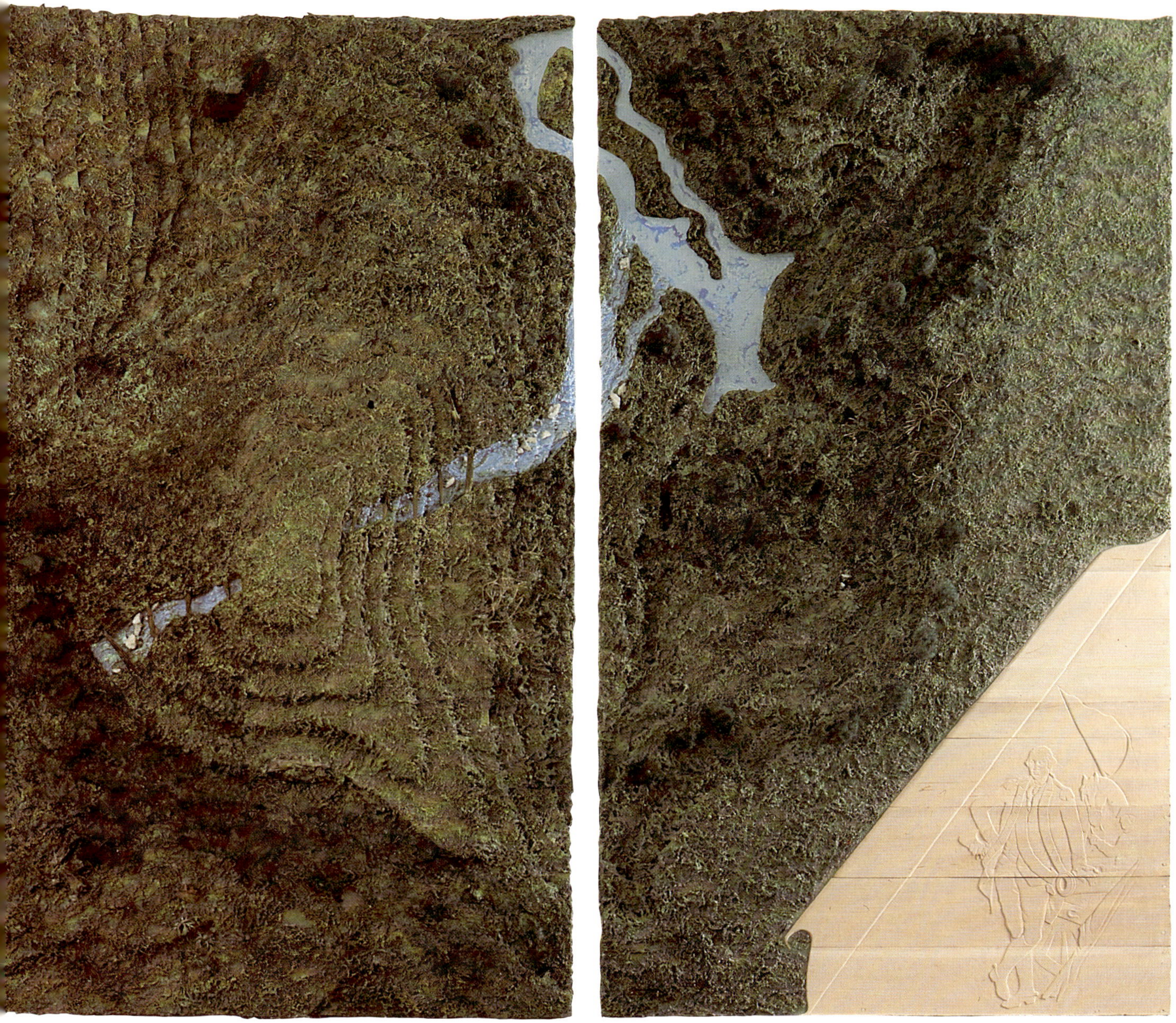

3. Wood and mixed media, 84 × 120 × 13″
Lent courtesy the artist

AN APPROXIMATE ORIGINAL CONTOUR

Artist's statement.

studies for steel cable tension/suspension structure in red, black and silver

This steel cable structure is based on the number expansion of Pascal's Triangle.

The number system represents a universal concept (the essence or nature of a thing), that becomes the vehicle through which analytical propositions are visualized (to visualize—to give form to—to create).

The network of numbers represents the "logic" that supports the structure, which itself represents "the system," and conversely, the system represents "structure."

The number logic reveals structural magnificence, as valid structuralization gives tribute to the basic beauty of logic. Underlying patterns and concept determine the form, while the logic remains intact.

Pattern-finding is the purpose of the mind and the construct of the universe. There is an infinite number of patterns, some of which are known; those that are still unknown hold the key to unsolved enigmas and paradoxes.

Thus formal and exclusively visual information can be refined to such an extent as to impart the most precise and significant information in addition to visual gratification.

This exercise in "visual mathematics" is a way of using universals and ultimates to arrive at true beginnings. (The formal cause—or—the cause of form).

As 3-d form, Systems of Logic has an almost invisible substructure to which the steel cables are attached and pulled taut, much like an inverted bridge with its supporting sides put end to end, while the sloping centers are suspended in mid air pointing at the viewer at both ends. The steel cables allow the entire network to be seen and the order, repetition and tension to be experienced.

In the vertical interpretation the structure can be seen from underneath and the cables converge at the top. As one looks up to the apex, the cables seem to be suspended from the clouds as they descend in a neat, tight formation around the viewer, like a tall, slim umbrella.

In the horizontal interpretation the effect is engineering and architectural tour-de-force. The viewer can walk around the cable network, experience the sharp tips staring at him head on (height about 6ft), while the designs created by the converging cables change relative to motion. A simple and pure interpretation of mathematics into form is quite evident.

In the vertical design the visual mathematics is also evident, but the strongest effect is not the tour-de-force, but that of being surrounded by the taut cables that seem to have a mind of their own. One is inside mathematics, almost controlled by it.

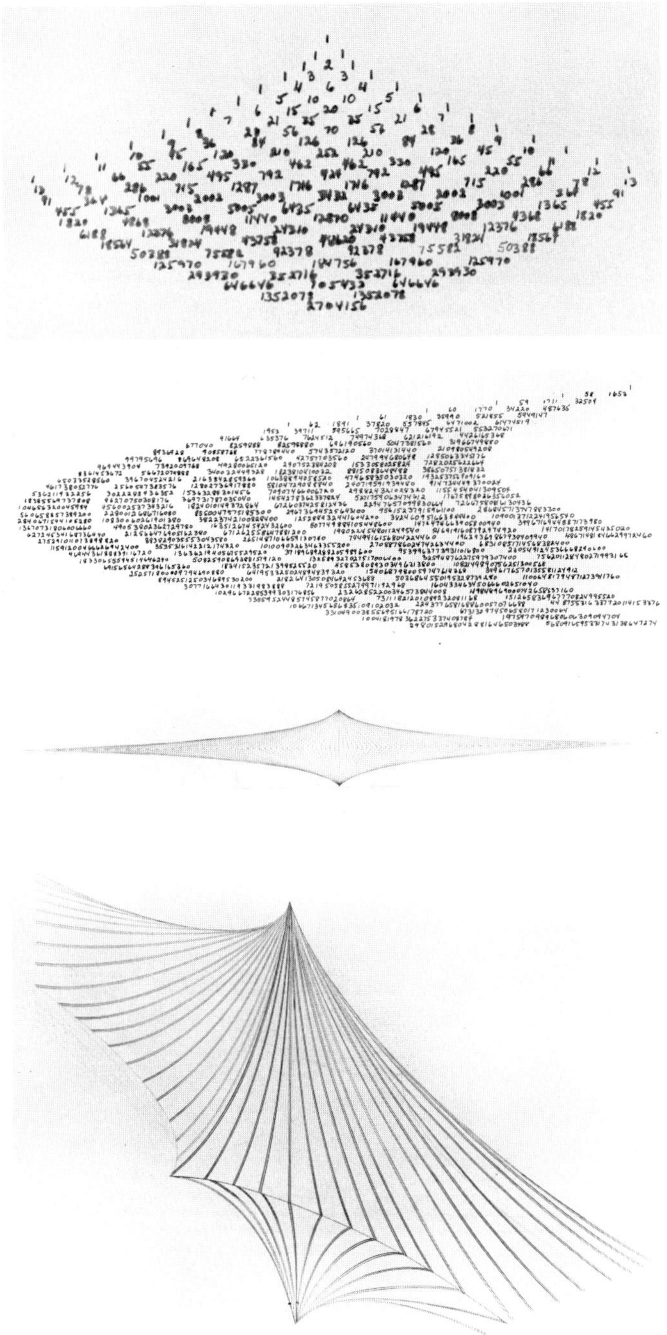

4A.

4A. Drawing—Study for steel cable structure in red, black, and silver. Ink on mylar, 108 × 30⅛″. Details
4B. Drawing—Studies for steel cable structure in red, black, and silver. Ink and pencil on mylar, 34¼ × 67⅛″
Lent courtesy the artist and Germans VanEck Gallery, New York

PASCAL'S TRIANGLE
Systems of Logic/Logic of Systems

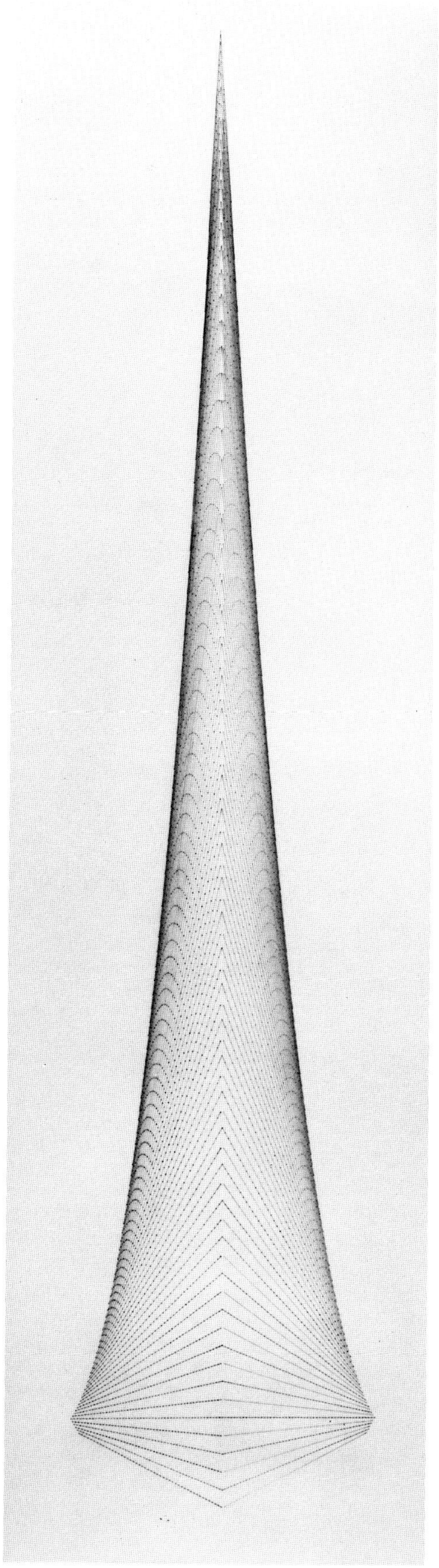

4B.

5A.

5B.

5C.

5E.

5F.

5I.

5J.

Artist's statement. The ambient landscape serves as the background tableau against which this work choreographically narrates the story of the mythic Daphne, who, in an effort to elude Apollo, flees deeper and deeper into the woods, to be eventually turned into a tree. The myth itself can be read metaphorically as a gloss on the dichotomy between nature and culture. In the piece Daphne is seen in a Muybridge-like sequence of six positions along her flight's trajectory as it passes through a ravine and woods along a 2000 foot long dirt road horseshoeing around an open field. The positions catch Daphne in the course of her escape and transformation as she is bodily metamorphosed and spiritually converted from mortal to wood nymph—a process symbolized by the tree, her bush soul.

5) CAROLEE THEA

5D.

5G.

5H.

5K.

5L.

5M.

5A–M. Color xerox, collage, paint, 7 × 9″ each
Lent courtesy the artist

DAPHNE

Artist's statement. Four paths marked by metal stakes lead to the entrances of this multifaceted structure containing a stepped pool within its walls. The location is a clearing in a wooded area.

The walls act as filters between the exterior and the interior. A partial view of the interior is given through the slatted side; ladder-like elements provide a high lookout and a second glimpse of the inside; a covered walk is embedded in another wall. Layered walls fold in upon themselves on yet another side.

Points of entry are revealed as the structure is explored. Once inside, the pool is visible from a screened platform or elevated walkway. Concentric rings of water hold their position in this stepped pool.

The viewer moving into the structure is the connector between the interior and the exterior, the natural and built environments. The progression provides an accumulation of images, sequences of space. It is not a fixed scene. Images are suggested and simultaneously expended.

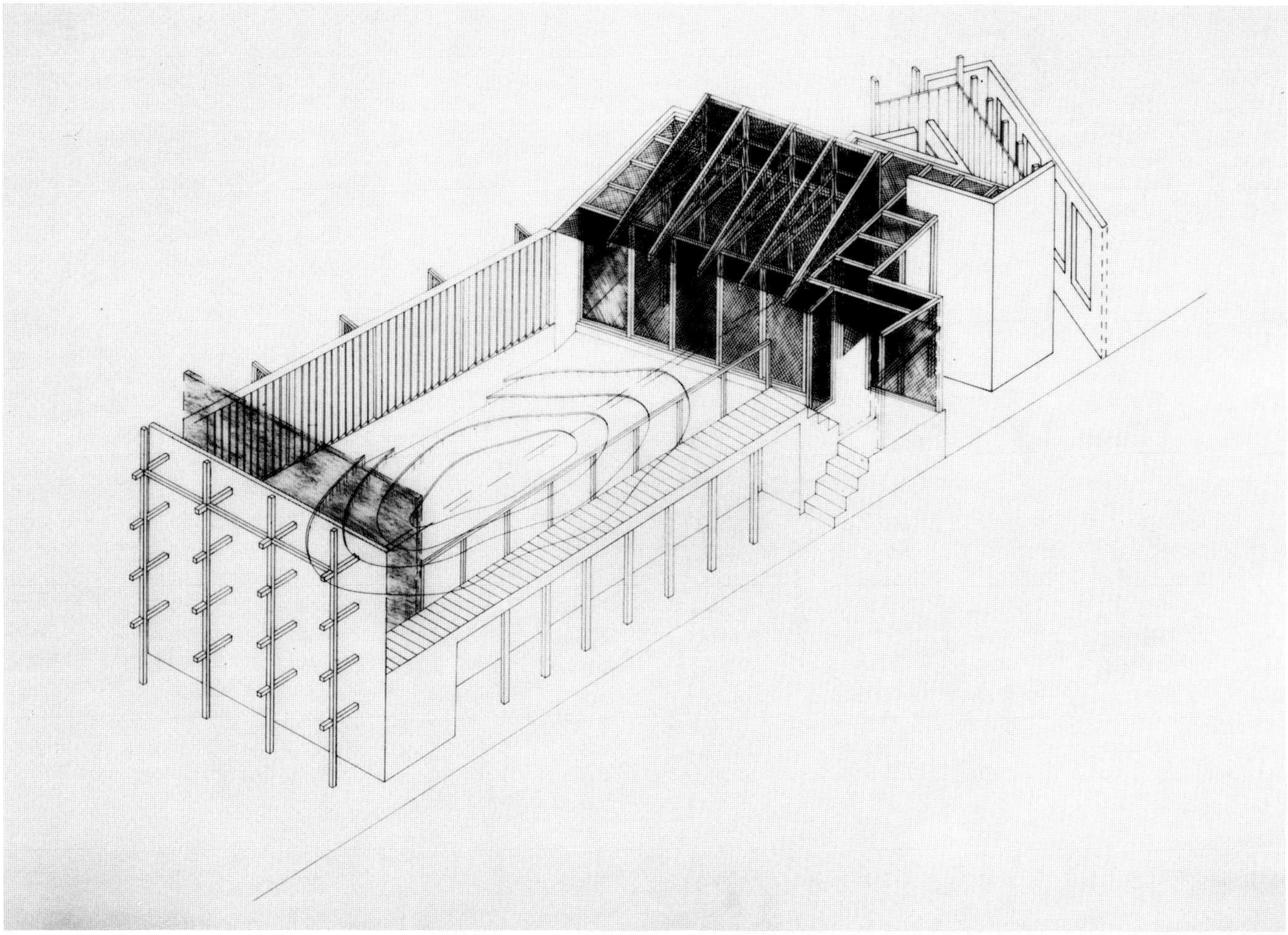

6. Ink on mylar, 38 × 51″
Lent courtesy Max Protech Gallery, New York

6) MARY MISS — STUDY FOR A COURTYARD: APPROACH TO A STEPPED POOL

7A.

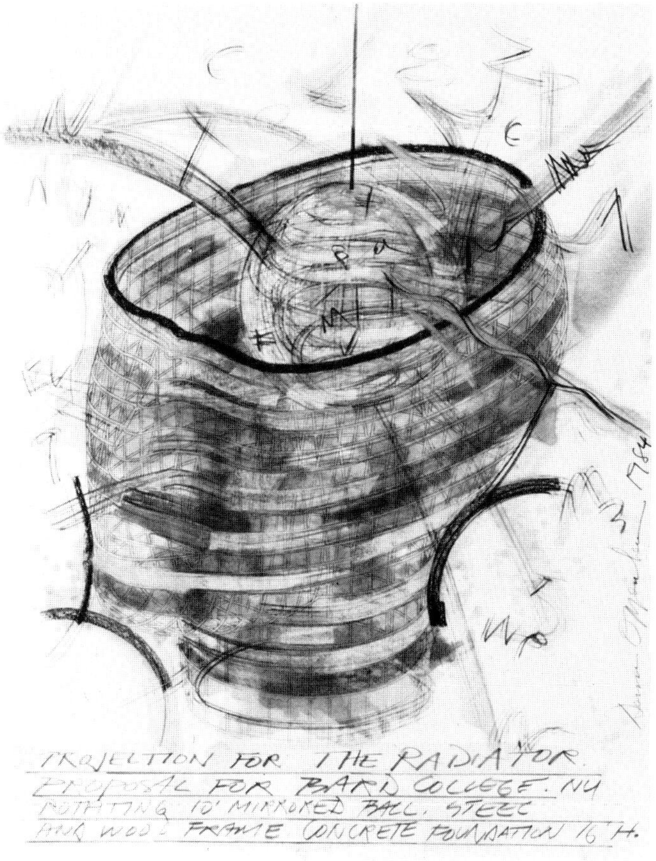

7B.

Artist's statement.

Radiator

This piece wants to address the spectator by employing a traditional image whereby one is invited to visually grasp the implications of a dynamic thought process which is not generally seen; i.e., a view of the creative process, the phenomenon of discovery. The activity within the mind's solar system is hinted at in a simple and coherent manner.

The piece could use outdoor spotlights at night, and the motor could turn the sphere at determined hours.

Dimensions: 14′H × 10′ in diameter

Materials: welded steel or marine plywood for head chamber, motorized glass ball, 8′ in diameter, ground based spotlights.

Method of construction: build head chamber, either in wood or welded steel, using templates for head ring sections, channel vertical space bars, fabricate motor mounts for glass ball, run electrical lines for spotlights and motor, fabricate sphere with mirrored panes, plant spotlights, concrete footings.

Labor and machine requirements: standard steel or wood shop for head chamber, professional fabricator for glass ball, engineer to design motor casings and determine positioning and type of motor, concrete footings for head chamber.

Maintenance: motor would require maintenance, dependent upon use.

Site: This piece should be best situated near a building, e.g. a library; however, site #10, in proximity to the art center, would be suitable.

(continued)

7A. **Radiator**
Scale model sculpture—aluminum, glass ball, rotating motor spotlight, 24 × 12″ diameter

7B. **Radiator**
Drawing—pencil, colored pencil, oil wash on paper, 38 × 50″

7C.

7E.

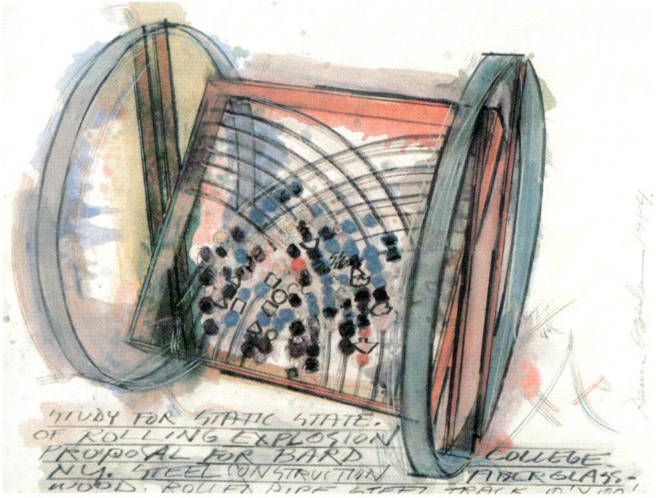

7D.

7F.

7C. **Rolling Explosion**
Scale model sculpture—hardwood, steel, aluminum, wooden beads, 24 × 24 × 10″

7D. **Rolling Explosion**
Drawing—pencil, colored paper, oil wash on paper, 38 × 50″

7E. **Woven Explosion (Mondrian Under Pressure)**
Scale model sculpture—galvanized steel, baked enamel, perforated aluminum, 30″diameter × 24″ high

7F. **Woven Explosion (Mondrian Under Pressure)**
Drawing—pencil, colored pencil, oil wash on paper, 50 × 38″

7) DENNIS OPPENHEIM, cont.

7G.

7H.

Rolling Explosion
This work depicts the configuration of a molecular explosion in the form of a mobile abacus that constantly radiates then contracts as it journeys along a track. The piece would remain stationary for the most part, but would be performed at certain pre-determined times.

Dimensions: 10′ OD steel rings, 7′W ×8′L aluminum frame, 50′-100′ steel track

Materials: (rings) ¼″ thick, 10″ steel channel with 2.5″ leg, rolled, leg out; (frame) ¼″ thick, 12″ aluminum channel with 2.5″ leg in; (internal tracks) 1″ OD aluminum tube, variable lengths solid poplar shapes, cut to specifications (could include real images, i.e., animals, trees, houses); (tracks) ¼″ thick, 8″ steel channel with 2.5″ leg up, ¼″ thick, 10″ H beams for track support, placed every 10′; concrete footings for H beams.

7G. **Roots in Cubism. Hearts in the Stars. (Forest for Cezanne)**
Scale model sculpture—marine plywood, tree trunk, galvanized steel arcs, boulder, 18 × 18″ diameter

7H. **Roots in Cubism. Hearts in the Stars. (Forest for Cezanne)**
Drawing—pencil, colored pencil, oil wash on paper, 38 × 50″
Lent courtesy the artist

Method of construction: build aluminum frame by bolting plates to corners, attach internal tracks using pipe fittings, bore holes through solid wooden shapes and slip through tube, close frame, weld ring sections into 10′ diameter rings, attach frame to cross section of two rings using heavy steel rod, weld feet onto channel tracks, pour footings, place track, place rubber scope on ends of track, lift main structure onto track.

Labor and machine requirements: factory to roll channel rings, steel cutting and welding shop, wood shop for solid shapes, concrete truck to pour footings, small crane or fork lift.

Maintenance needs: rust-preventive primer applied to all steel surfaces, wood stain for internal shapes.

Site: any open area with a low grade: site #6, #8, or #9.

Woven Explosion. (Mondrian under Pressure)
This piece builds upon three mushroom shape armatures in a decorative and spontaneous manner. It wants to capture a moment and depict a "frozen" state, in a sumptuous array of materials.

Dimensions: 12′H × 10′ in diameter

Materials: three rolled steel "mushroom" armatures, made in ¼″ thick, 4″ plate steel, central rod in heavy gauge steel, galvanized steel, baked enamel, perforated steel, expanded steel, fiberglass, concrete foundation.

(statement continues, p. 52)

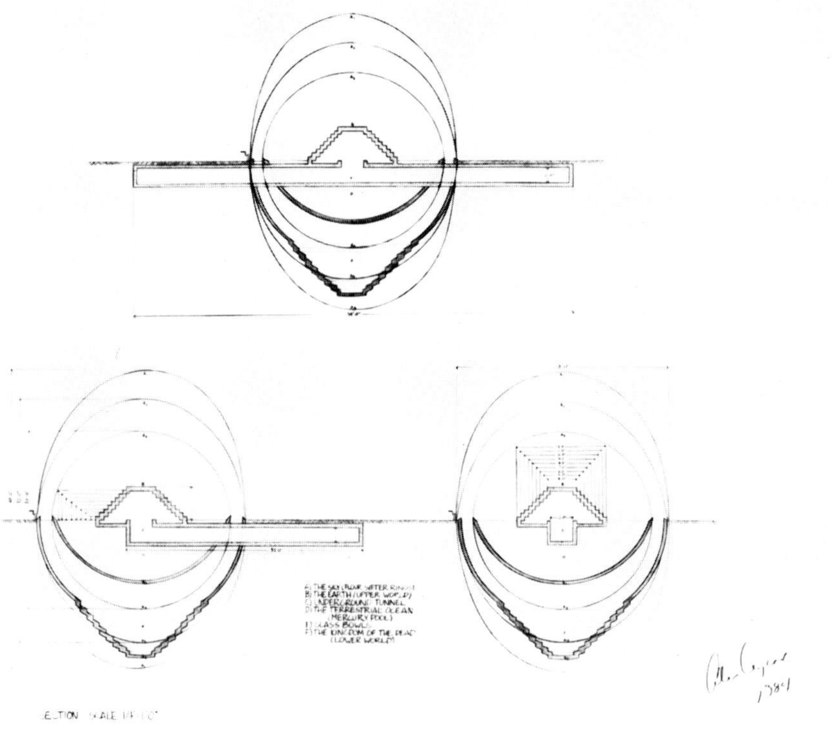

8A.

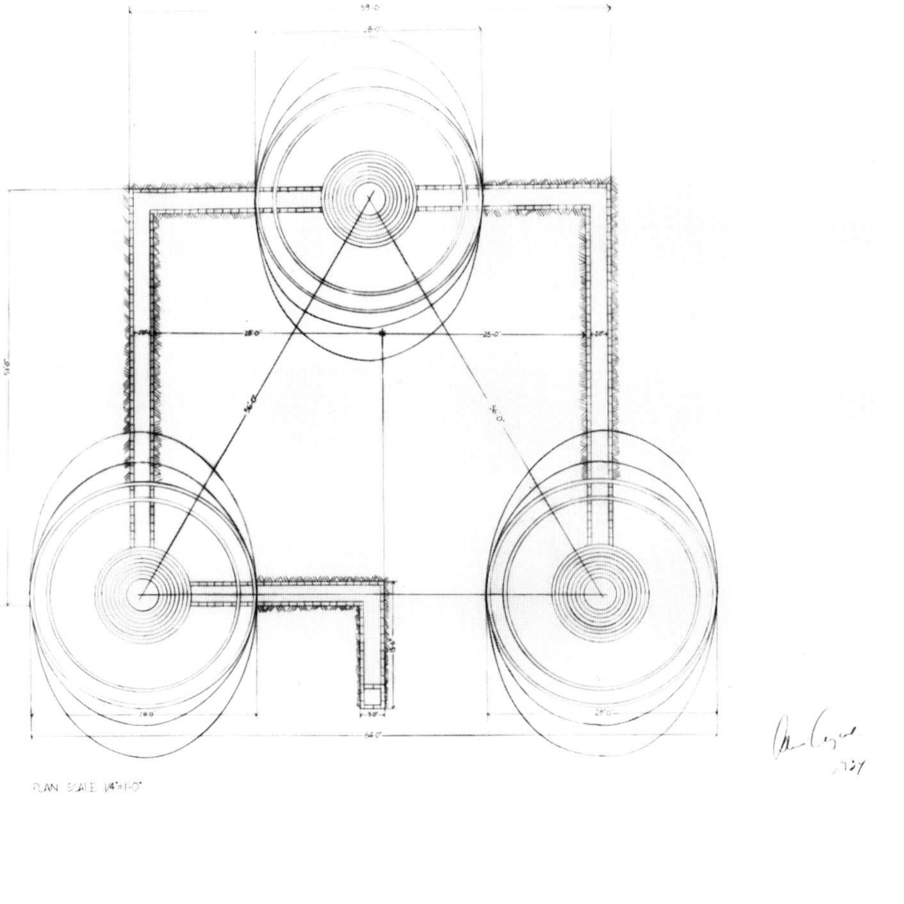

8B.

8) ALICE AYCOCK

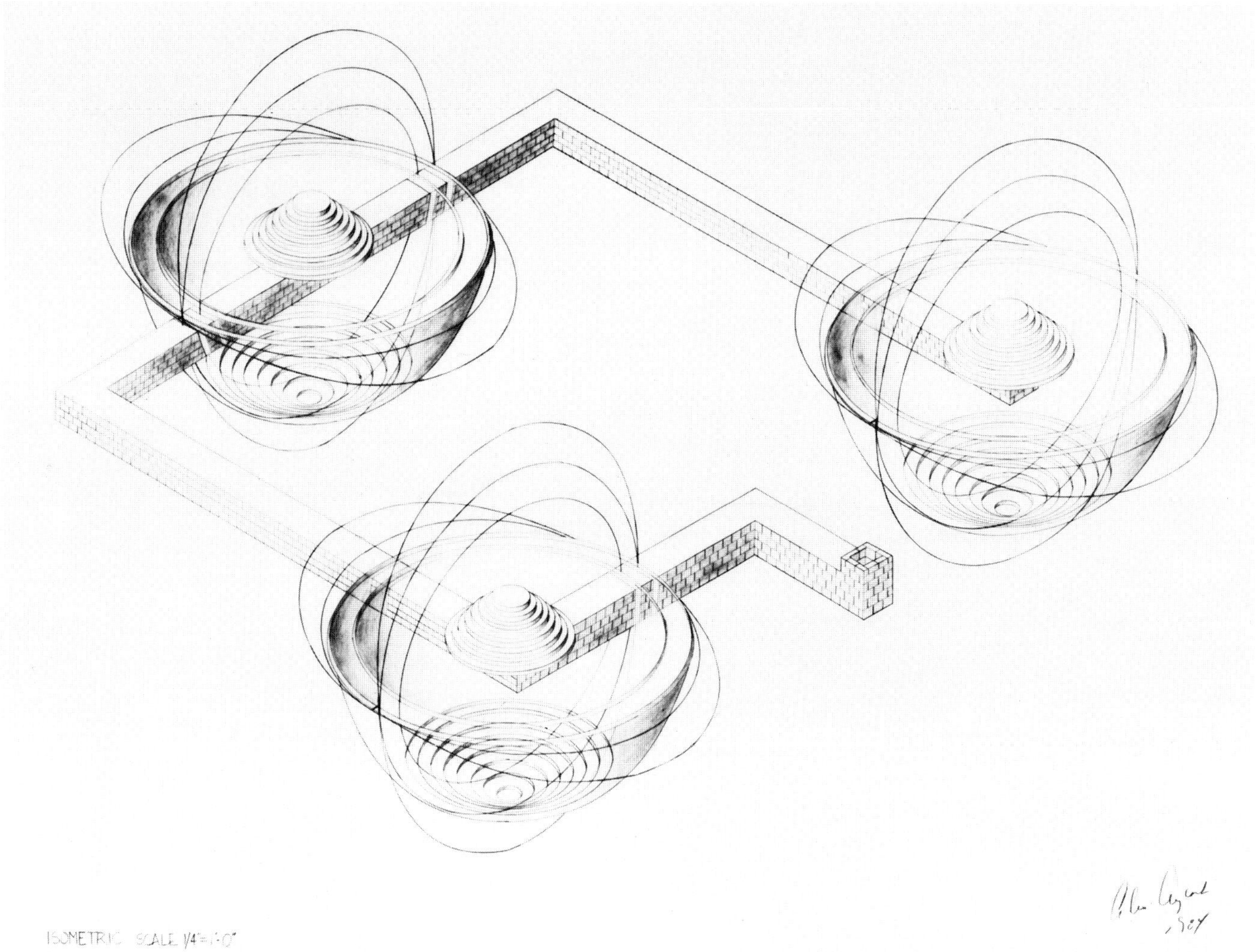

8C.

Artist's statement. Build three identical schematic models of the world. For each model, set two concentric glass bowls, 24 ft. and 28 ft. in diameter, separated by water, into the ground. The innermost bowl (the Terrestrial Ocean) is filled with mercury. A stepped, concentric, hollow concrete island (the Earth), 12 ft. in diameter and 4½ ft. high, rests in the ocean of mercury. At the bottom of the outermost glass, concentrically stepped bow lies the Kingdom of the Dead, (the Underworld). Three concentric rings (The Flour Sifter) rotate on an axis perpendicular to the plane of the mercury pool and ground. The largest ring, passing 20 ft. above the ground, cuts 20 ft. through the ground; the middle ring, passing 16 ft. above and below, cuts through the Underworld; and the smallest ring, passing 10 ft. above and below, cuts between the Terrestrial Ocean and the Underworld. One is able to move from concrete chamber to concrete chamber through an underground tunnel with an interior space of 2 ft. high and wide.

8A. Drawing—pencil on mylar, 27 × 34″
8B. Drawing—pencil on mylar, 27 × 34″
8C. Drawing—pencil on mylar, 27 × 34″
Lent courtesy the artist

A REPRESENTATION OF THE SECOND WORLD
(from "Three Concrete Chambers" Series)

Artist's statement.

Free-standing parts:

20′ × 28′ × 14½′	stainless steel and corten steel
19½′ × 24′ × 12′	stainless steel
10′ × 20′ × 6½′	corten
11′ × 20½′ × 20′	corten
6½′ × 11′ × ¼″	corten
16½′ × 20′ × 6′	corten
16½′ × 18′ × 8′	corten
18½′ × 14′ × 9′	corten
15′ × 18′ × 9′	stainless steel

Intention

Sculptures, the forms of which may evoke field and mountain, tree and cloud, as well as fire, water, and wind, speak to the viewer of the world around him. Using industrial steel and machines to create these forms, and industrial chemicals to pit and destroy them, may introduce a metaphor for the possibility of harmony between the demands of our industrial society and nature, and, at the same time, sound the alarm of the fragile quality of that relationship. The brooding presence of the great forms in the proposed piece, TRANS-12, may reflect the anxiety, terrible and overwhelming, that this relationship of technology and nature brings, the fear of loss—loss of civilization and livelihood, indeed of life, if the delicate balance is not guarded, watched and maintained.

Proposal

The sculpture, of 9 free-standing parts, will be situated on the flat area of the slight rise of ground in the field across from the Edith C. Blum Art Institute (see topographical map) on an area approximately 60′ × 84′. The elements of the sculpture will be constructed of welded mill finish stainless steel and of corten steel (cut from 20′ sheets of ¼″, ½″ and 10 gauge). Cement and reinforcing rod footings 2′ wide and 4′ deep will be sunk in the ground to follow the contours under the bases of each piece. Upon installation, each piece will be bolted to these footings. A portable traveling hoist will be necessary to move, raise and place the elements of the sculpture over the footings. Soil displaced in digging the footings will be smoothed over the footings, and wild grasses and weeds will grow up around the bases of the sculpture. No bases—no artificial visual barriers between the sculptural forms and the earth—will exist.

Because of the dimensions of this work, it must be constructed in a large industrial space equipped with adequate electric power, grabbers, chains and lifts, preferably at Malruble, Bethany, Connecticut. The sculptor and one experienced assistant can do the work. However, an installation crew from Bill Giza at Malruble should install it.

Heavy duty cutters, knibblers, grinders, grinding and sanding wheels, an industrial arc welder and appropriate rods, an argon welder, oxy-acetylene cutting torch and tanks of gas, a metal punch capable of handling ½″ plate, and a steel brake capable of handling 20′ sheets of ½″ steel will be used for constructing this work. The pieces will be cut and welded. The design calls for standard 20′ × 8′ sheets of steel to be used

(statement continues, p. 52)

9) BEATRICE PERRY

9. Miniature—welded steel, 10 × 30 × 44″
Lent courtesy the artist

TRANS 12

PURE WATER STILL A PROPOSAL FOR BARD COLLEGE

STILL PURE WATER IS A WORK OF SCULPTURE THAT STORES WARMTH AND YIELDS PURE WATER. THE WORK IS TO BE SITED FROM NORTH TO SOUTH AT THE HIGHEST ELEVATION ON THE FIELD (139.5') SO THAT THE WATER ON ITS DOWNWARD FLOW WILL HAVE SUFFICIENT PRESSURE TO RISE TO THE LEVEL OF THE SPIGOT IN THE GALLERY. OTHER SITES ARE ALSO FEASIBLE. FOR INSTANCE, AN ALTERNATE CONSTRUCTION MIGHT SITE THIS PIECE MUCH CLOSER TO THE GALLERY AND MAKE IT 5 FEET HIGHER.

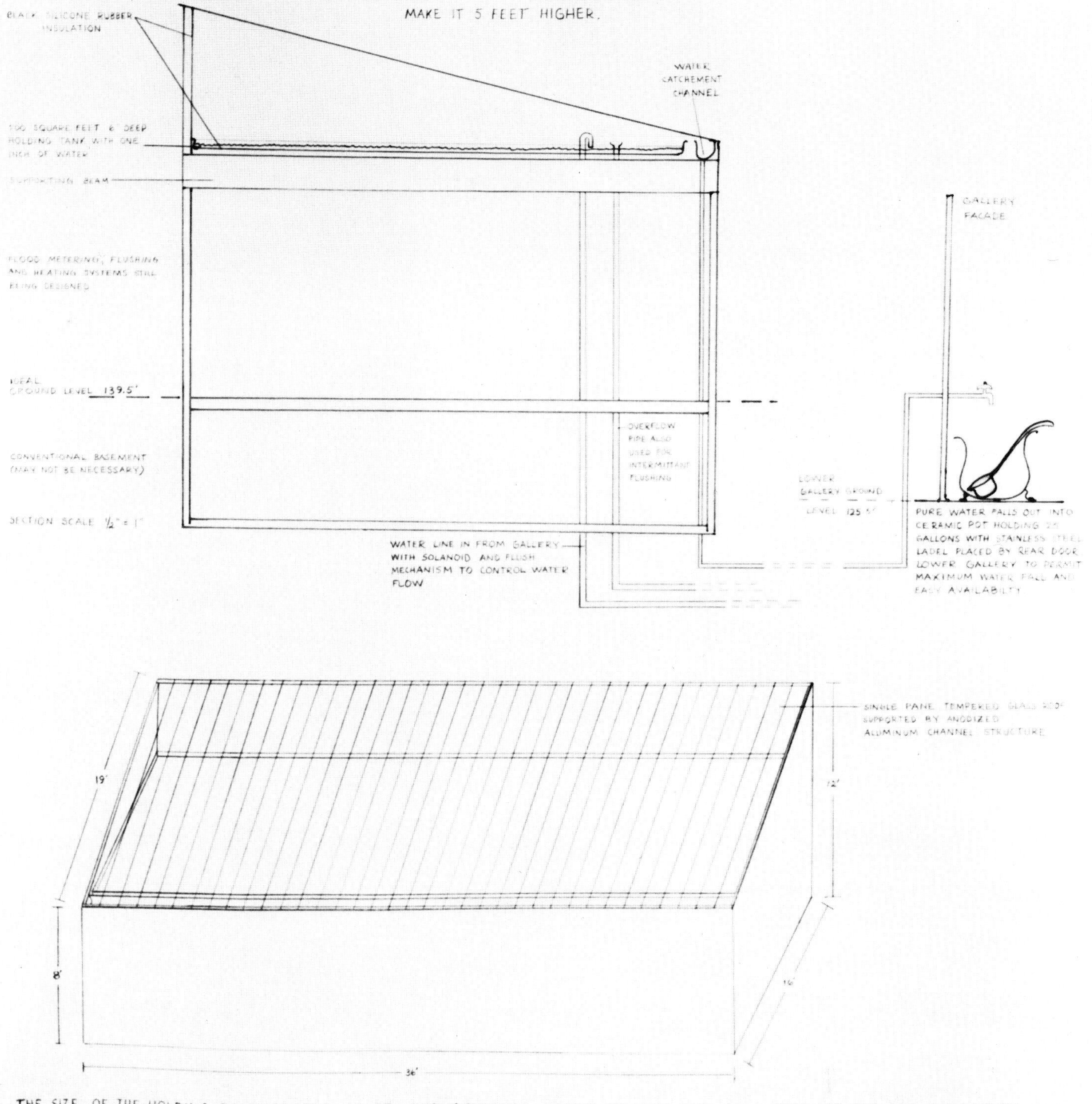

THE SIZE OF THE HOLDING TANK IS 500 SQ. FT. AND CONTAINS ABOUT 25 GALLONS OF WATER AT THE ONE INCH LEVEL. WE ASSUME 10 TO 20 GALLONS A DAY WILL CONDENSE ON THE GLASS ROOF AND THEREAFTER MOVE THROUGH THE SYSTEM.

10) HELEN AND NEWTON HARRISON (with Joshua Harrison and Bettina Marks)

WHY DO IT AT ALL?

AS ANYONE CAN SEE THERE IS A BROWN RESIDUE INSIDE THE TEAPOT

WHERE WOULD YOU PUT IT?

BETWEEN HERE AND THERE WITH THE ROOF PLANE FACING SOUTH

DOES IT MATTER HOW FAR?

AS LONG AS THE PIPES CAN REACH

HOW BIG SHOULD IT BE?

BIG ENOUGH TO YIELD SEVERAL HUNDRED DRINKS

HOW BIG IS A DRINK?

BETWEEN A CUP AND A SWALLOW

HOW TALL SHOULD IT BE?

TALL ENOUGH FOR WATER TO SEEK ITS OWN LEVEL

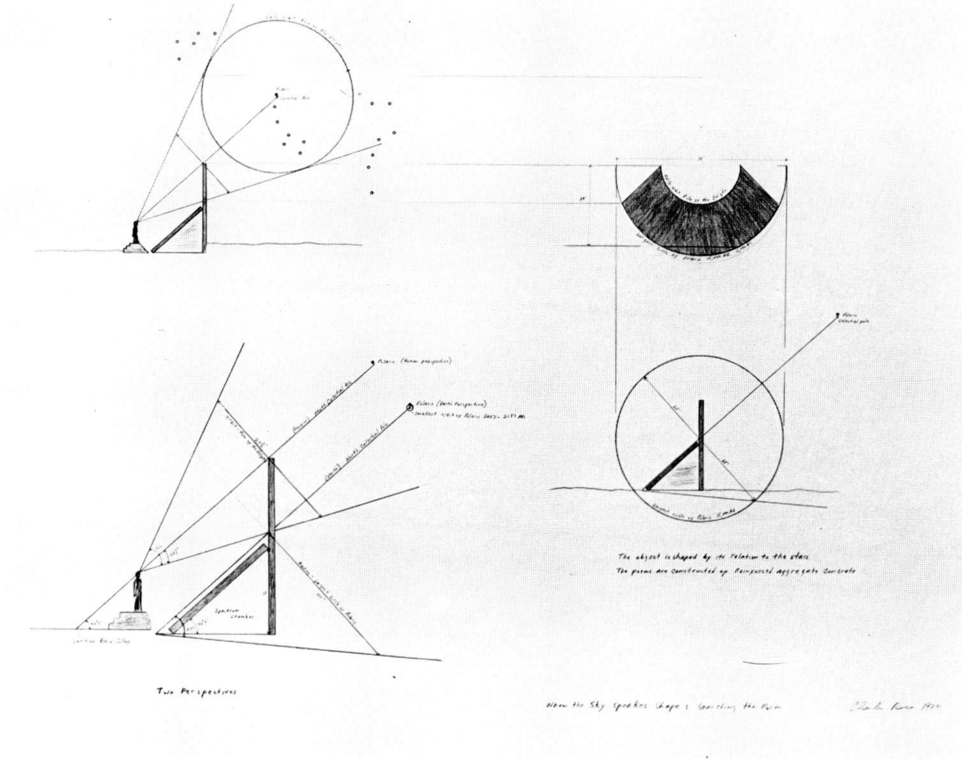

11A.

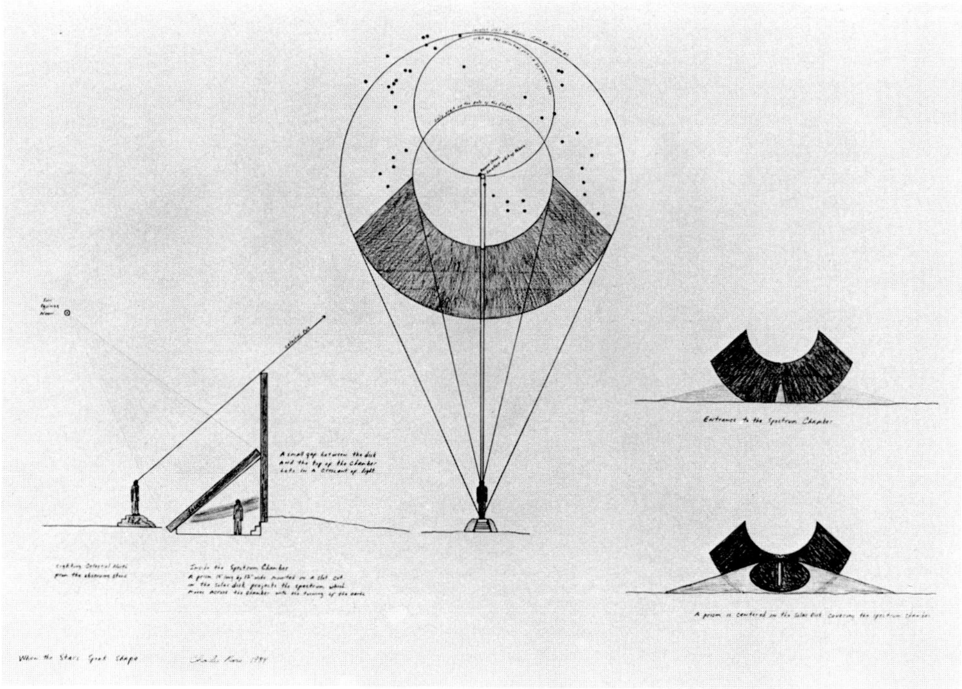

11B.

11) CHARLES ROSS

11C.

Artist's statement. When the stars speak shape, the form in earth, light, and concrete.

11A. **When the Stars Speak Shape**
Drawing—ink, pastel, pencil on paper, 30½ × 44¼″
11B. **When the Stars Speak Shape: Searching the Form**
Drawing, 30½ × 41″
11C. **When the Stars Speak Shape**
Model—wood prism, marble paste, volcanic rock,
19 × 36 × 11″
Lent courtesy the artist

WHEN THE STARS SPEAK SHAPE

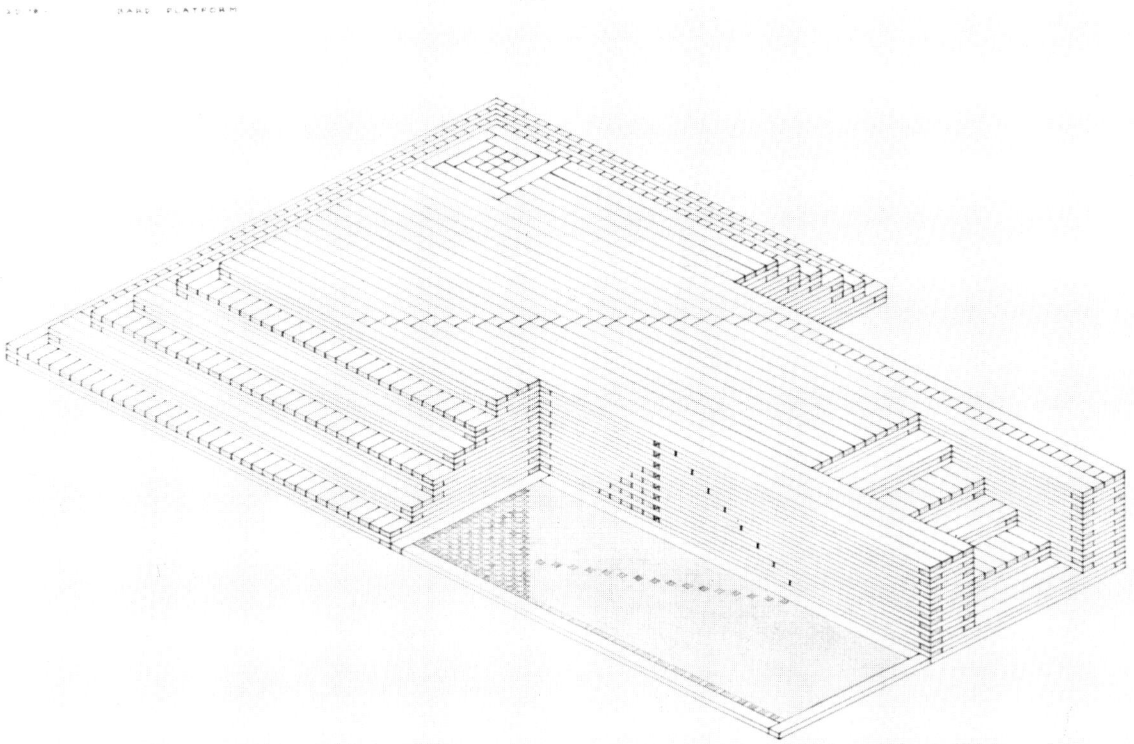

12A.

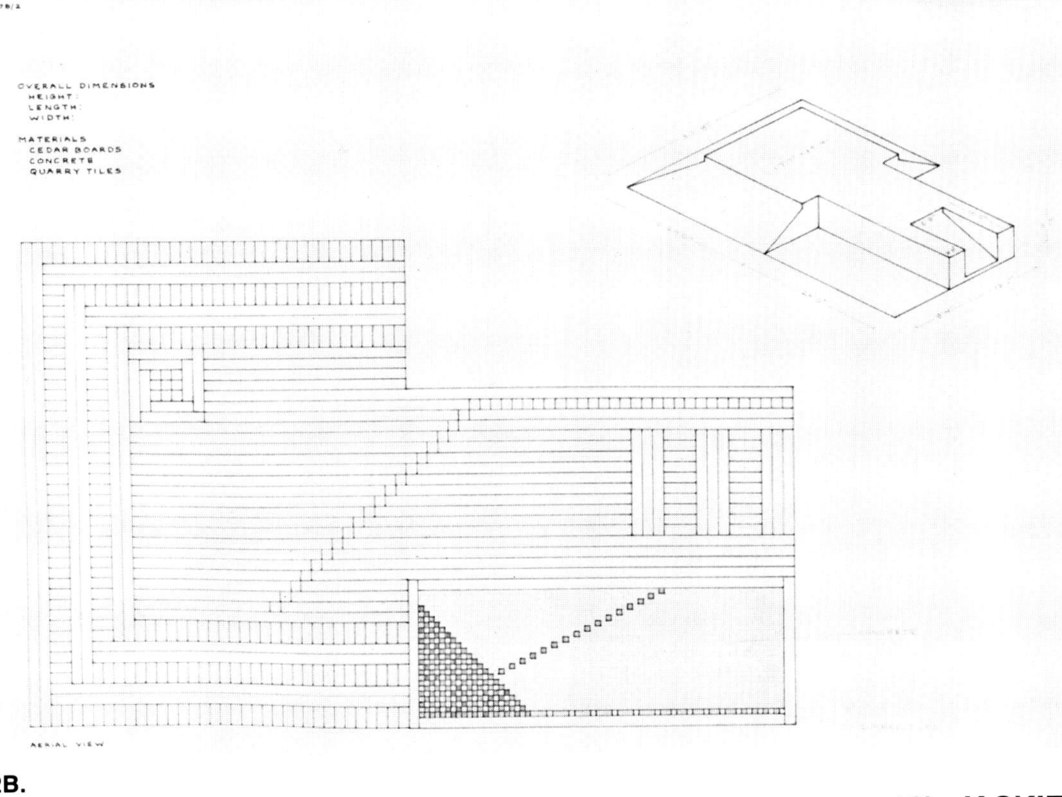

12B.

12) JACKIE FERRARA

Artist's statement. The Bard Platform is designed to serve two functions:

1. A visual experience that alters upon climbing the platform. From above there will be a difference in the viewer's perception of the piece. For example, the interaction of the two "floor" surfaces (that is, the concrete deck and the platform top) is not visible from the ground level.

2. A platform stage for performances. In addition to the top area there is the potential of using the steps and concrete deck as well.

Dimensions
Overall: 6′0″ high by 48′0″ long by 30′8″ wide.
Top surface: 41′4″ long by 17′4″ wide.

Materials
Structure: cedar boards 4″ by 8″ of varying lengths; lag bolts.
Deck: concrete; quarry tiles; cedar casing.

Method of construction
Structure: Prior to delivery the boards are cut to size at the lumber yard. All construction occurs at the site. Boards are secured by bolting each one in at least two places to the one below.
Deck: Concrete is mixed and poured. While it is still wet the quarry tiles are set into place.

Labor and machine requirements
4 construction workers
2 masons
concrete mixer

Maintenance needs
None required except, if desired, an occasional hosing or sweeping.

12A. Pencil and ink on paper, 17 × 22″
12B. Pencil and ink on paper, 17 × 22″
Lent courtesy Max Protech Gallery, New York

2-D 78 BARD PLATFORM

13. Model—wood, stone, earth, 20 × 36½ × 60″
Lent courtesy the artist

13) MICHAEL SINGER

Artist's statement. My proposal for the Bard Campus involves creating a trail from the cultivated field down through the wooded ravine. There is a stream that runs through this ravine. At the bottom, in the flat area indicated, the wooden structure will be built, creating a shelter for the viewer to enter. In the structure is a raised earthen floor with stones.

(detail of interior)

PROPOSAL FOR BARD COLLEGE

Artist's statement.

1. Catherine Wheel—
   Catherine of Alexandria AD 307, Christian Martyr
   A wheel with spikes projecting from the rim
   A pinwheel
   Cartwheel
2. Wheel—
   A moving or essential part of something likened to a machine
3. The first step, origins, earthen hut, first urban plan
4. Wheeling in its tracks

Five Spoke Seeded Catherine Wheel—overview of "wheel"—layout of wood treated roof and interior structure and roof support. Entire wall structure of "seeded Catherine wheel" is cracked face cement block and is seeded. All spoke corridors have two openings. Rot treated timber cut and spaced to allow light and drainage—earth and seed filled on top of timber roof on corridors and wheel.

Speaking in Tongues Project Series: *Tower for the Study of Languages:* Entire structure of timber reinforced with angle iron in the interior—tongues of wood lathing with angle iron armatures. Timber for Tower is spaced to allow light inside. Four small lofts fastened to interior walls act as "study porches" at different heights. Tongues on sides of tower are 2½′ × 3′, 3½′ × 5′. "Hoist" and chair on cable are stationary.

Five Spoke Seeded Catherine Wheel

Dimensions: Wheel—20′W × 7′H; spokes—45′L Each × 7′H.

Materials: Seed, soil, cracked face block, angle iron, timber.

Construction: Concrete running channel foundation for entire structure 24″ deep. For axel tower foundation concrete 48″ deep. Block to be mortared.

Labor and Machine: Crew of 4, cement mixer, welding equipment, generator.

Maintenance: Seeding and watering first few weeks, then nothing.

Axel Tower and Seeded Catherine Wheel

Dimensions: Tower—35′H × 12½′ at base; wheel—20′W × 7′H; spokes—45′L Each × 7′H.

Materials: Seed, soil, cracked face cement block, angle iron, timber, glass.

(statement continues, pg. 53)

14A.

14) JODY PINTO

14B.

14C.

14A. **Five Spoke Seeded Catherine Wheel**
Graphite on paper, 30 × 40″
14B. **Axel Tower and Seeded Catherine Wheel**
Graphite on paper, 30 × 40″
14C. **Speaking in Tongues Project Series: Tower for the Study of Languages**
Graphite on paper, 36 × 59″
Lent courtesy Hal Bromm Gallery, New York

PROPOSALS FOR LAND MARKS PROJECT

Artist's statement.

Endless Column: Tree fragments from all over the U.S.A. as well as fragments from the Bard area. Fallen fragments of forests that have been collected nationwide. Each fragment represents a native tree of each location. (cast in bronze)

Tower of Leaves: A sculpture showing the recycling process of leaves collected from the forest surrounding the site of Bard College.

Circle of Life: A cross section of the forest of the Bard area (6′ wide forming a circle) showing the complete cycle of the forest with a rising hill in the center. On the rise within the hill will be placed a series of columns of bronze fragments of the fallen limbs within Bard's forest.

15A.

(detail of Circle of Life)

15) ALAN SONFIST

15B.

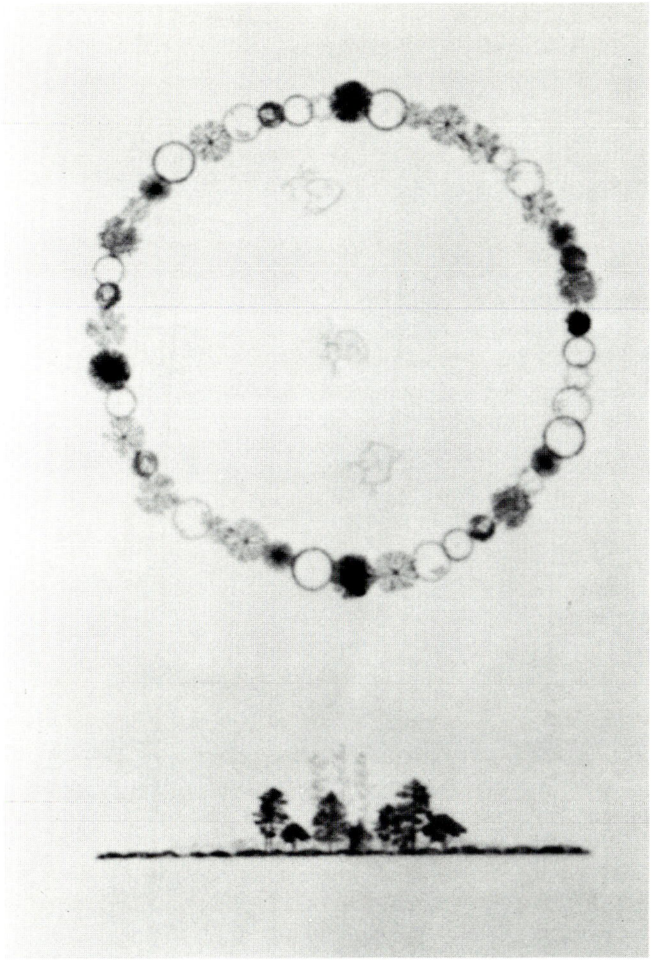

15C.

15A. **Endless Columns of Limbs**
Pastel and pencil on paper, 44 × 30″
15B. **Tower of Leaves**
Pastel and pencil on paper, 44 × 30″
15C. **Circle of Life**
Pastel and pencil on paper, 44 × 33″
Lent courtesy the artist

WORKS IN NATURE'S MATERIALS FOR LAND MARKS PROJECT

Artist's statement. The untitled granite block project for Bard College is one of a series of site specific projects, with constructed block elements, with which I've been involved. Once I determined the basic gesture of the proposal, I worked with a full size set of wooden blocks to resolve the actual sculpture. The construction, primarily horizontal, would be a destination and place within the field.

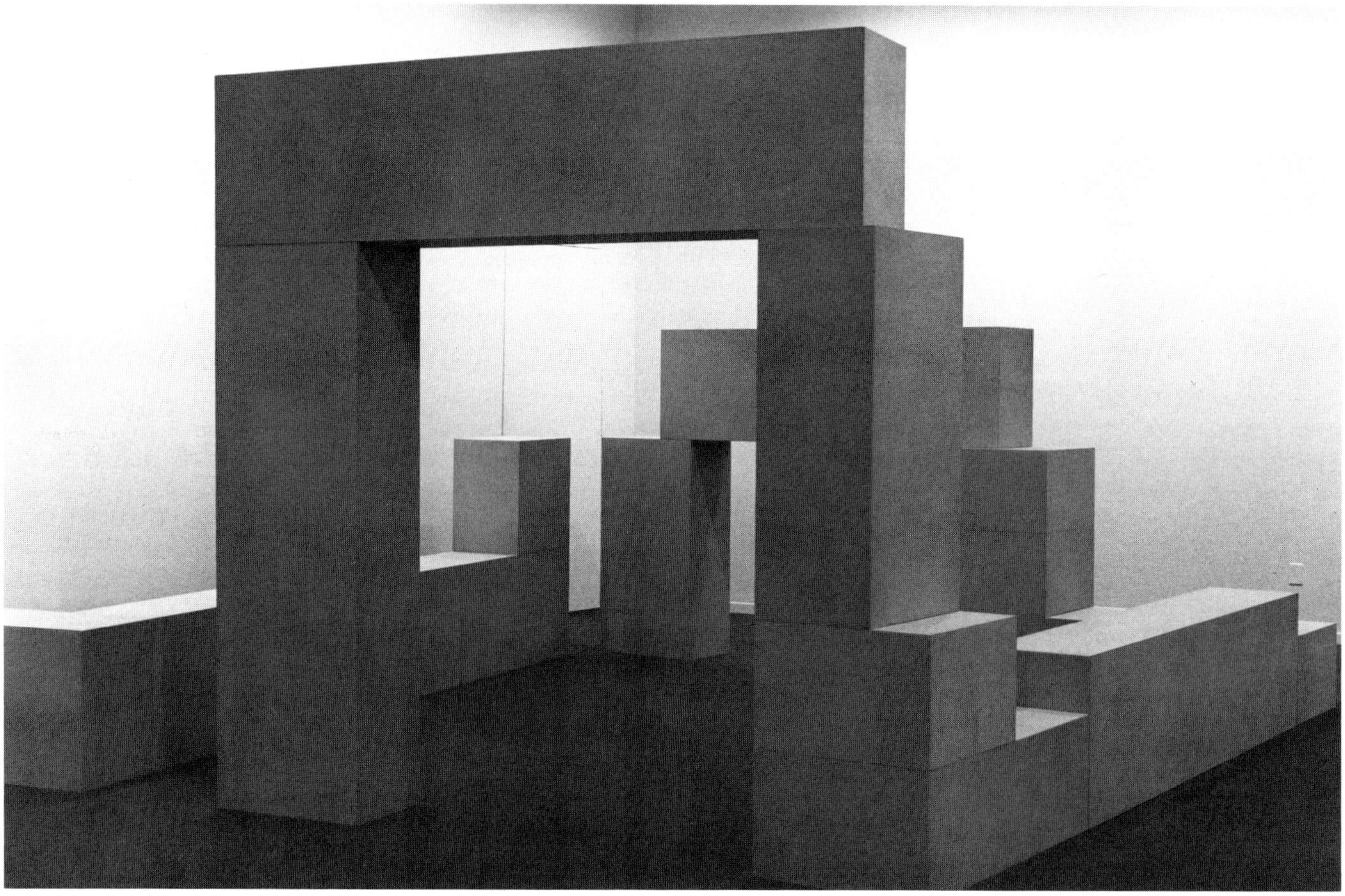

16A.

16) RICHARD FLEISCHNER

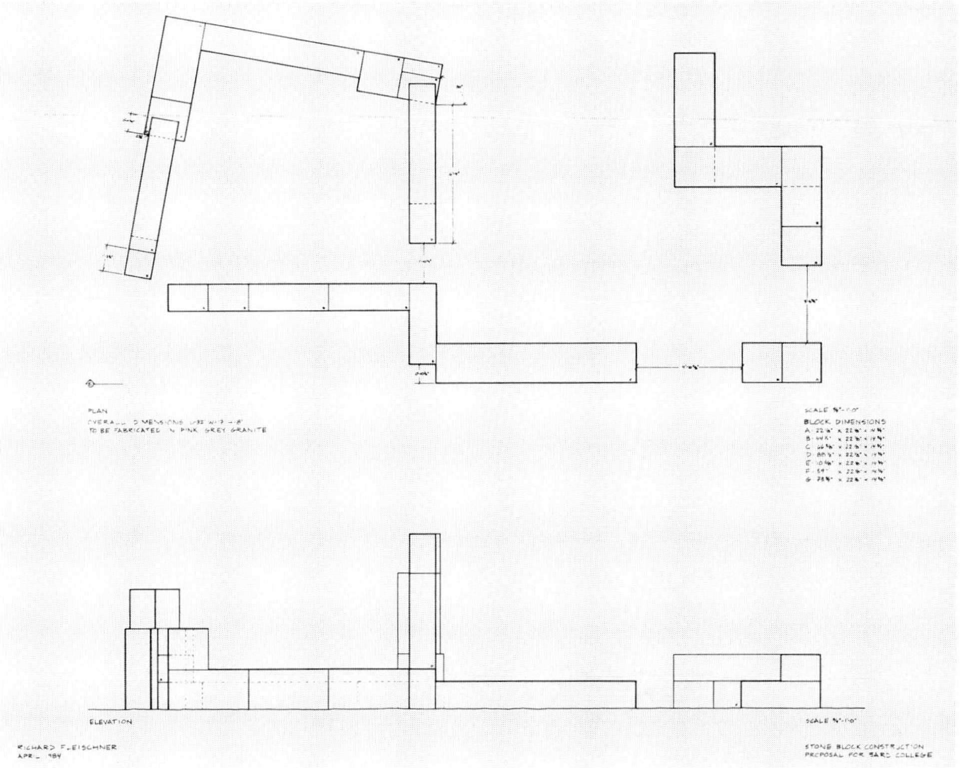

16B.

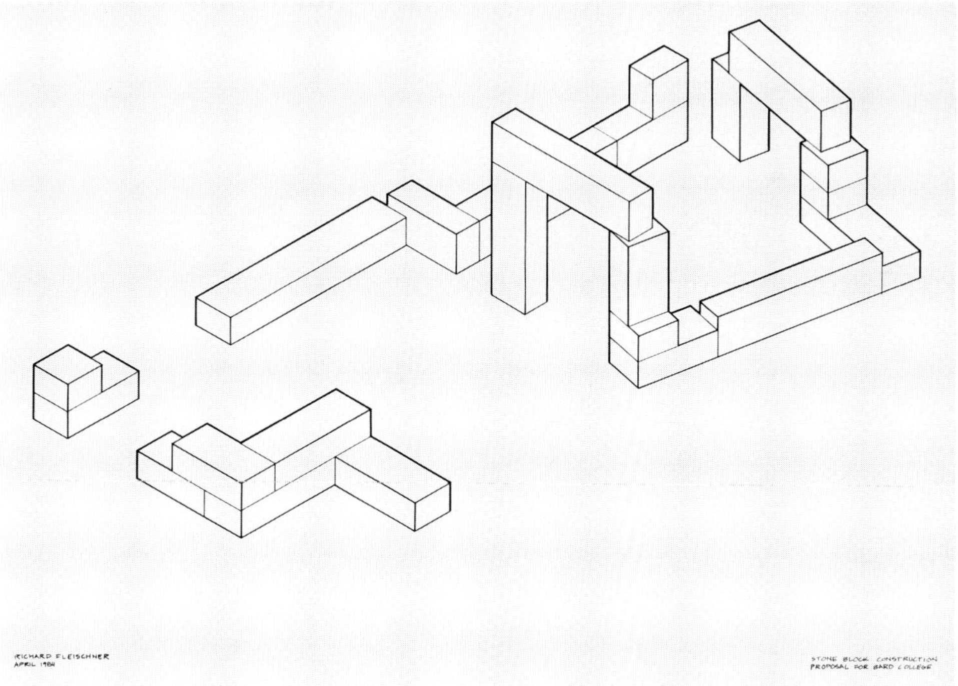

16C.

16A. Diazo print and xerox print, 28 × 41″
16B. Diazo print and xerox print, 28 × 41″
16C. Diazo print and xerox print, 28 × 41″
Lent courtesy the artist

STONE BLOCK WOOD CONSTRUCTION
(pink grey granite)

Artist's statement. Normally there are cost ceilings for my outdoor projects. The "Land Marks" exhibition has no restrictions on the size of the work or its cost. I had no idea how difficult an unlimited project could be. Could it be bronze? or as large as I wanted it to be? I had to give myself a lower budget and settled on cast aluminum and a smaller scale. What I ended up with is a structure related to ships; abandoned, wrecked, a graveyard of Hudson River history.

(detail)

17) ROBERT STACKHOUSE

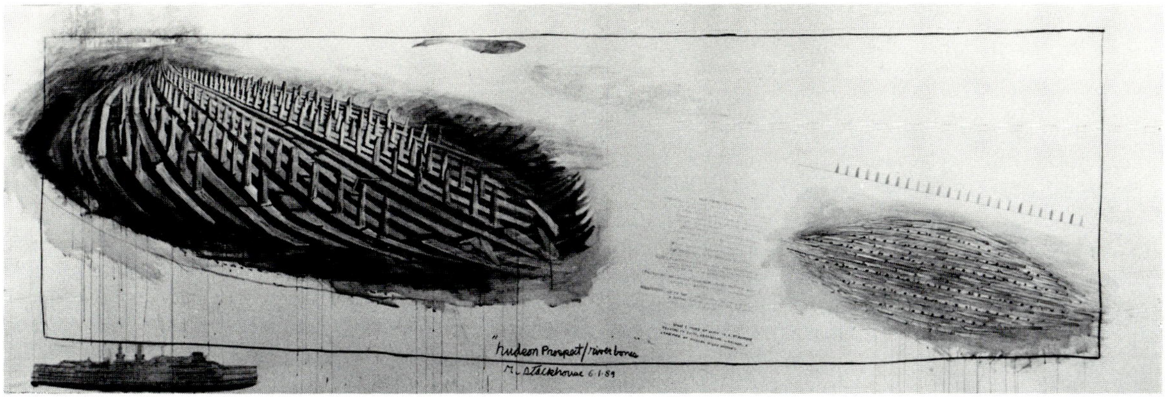

17.

17. Watercolor on paper, 60 × 183″
Lent courtesy of Max Hutchinson Gallery, New York

HUDSON PROSPECT/RIVER BONES

Artist's statement. The architectural structures of **O Silo** were inspired by the concrete stave silo with its ribbed steel dome and central circular opening. I visited silos of this type in the countryside surrounding Bard.

From the "viewing platform" ninety feet above the ground at the top of the tallest silo structure, the Hudson River, which is normally obscured by the trees, can be seen coursing through the landscape. The campus and towns along the river will also come into view.

The various structures of **O Silo,** along with many of their apertures, are aligned with the sunsets and sunrises on the summer and winter solstices and the equinoxes, and with the North-South axis. They will come into visual alignment from the "viewing platform."

There are several subterranean chambers and a long tunnel sloping into a sunken silo, which makes descending below as much a part of experiencing this work as climbing to the heights. From below, looking up, a circle of sky will be seen. Looking down through the hole in the domes of the lower structures, a circle of ground, sometimes with a circle of light illuminating it, will come into view.

18A.

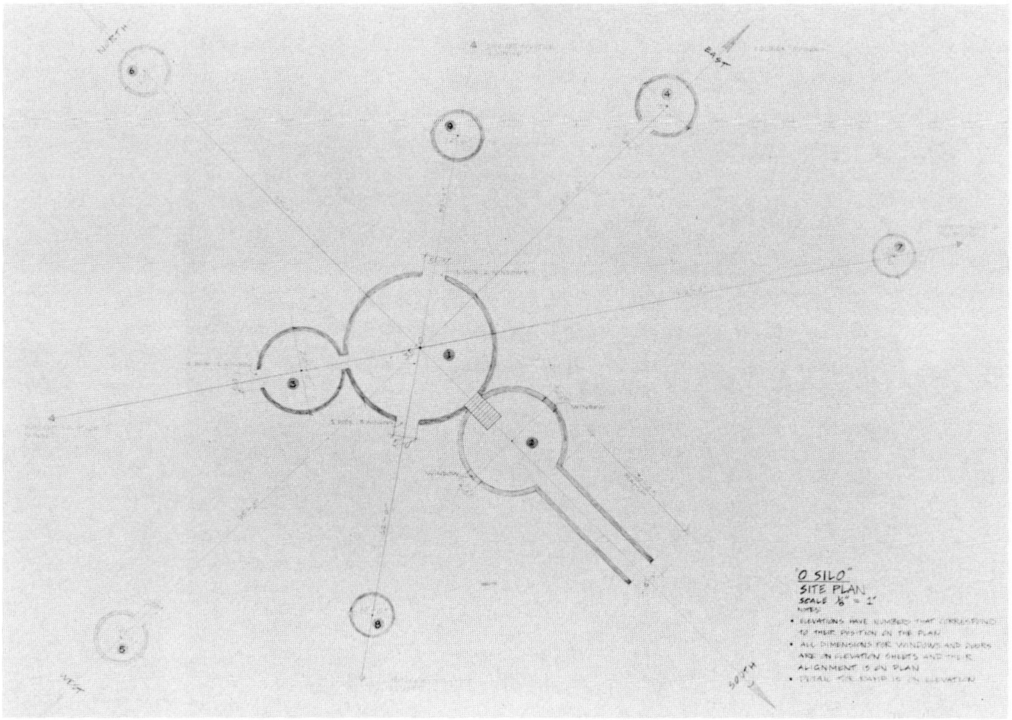

18B.

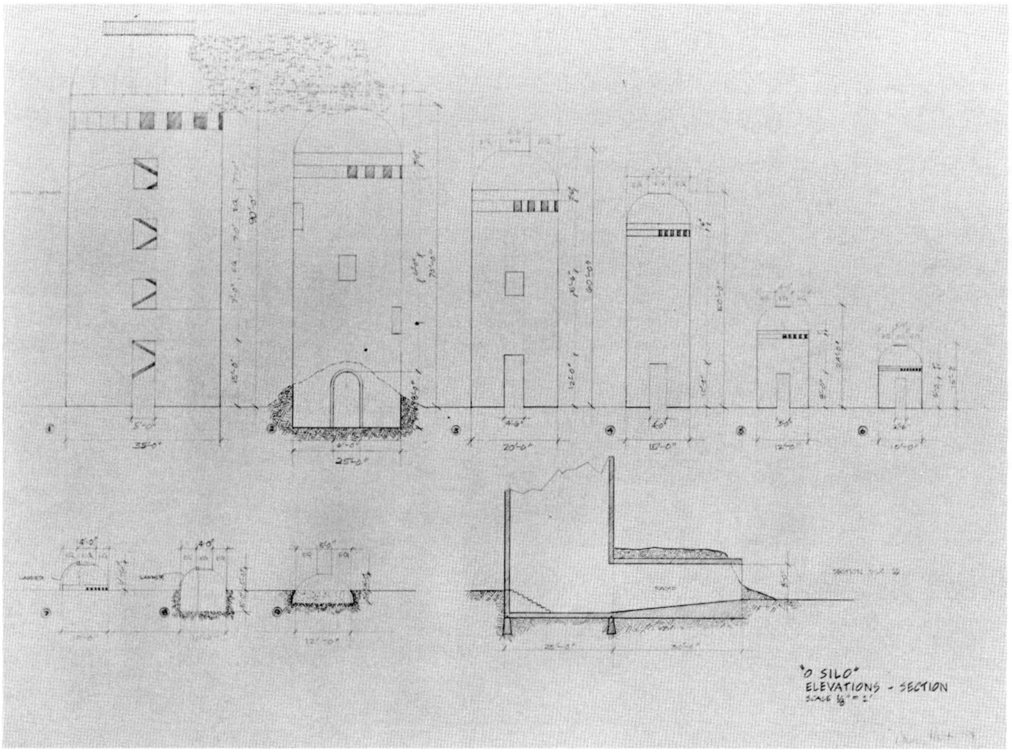

18C.

18A. Model—wood, cardboard, aluminum, 12 × 30 × 36″
18B. Drawing—pencil on paper, 22 × 30″
18C. Drawing—pencil on paper, 22 × 30″
Lent courtesy John Weber Gallery, New York

O SILO

19A.

Artist's statement. One hopes that students in whatever field they choose, will be the poets of their time and maybe for all time. One praises the book . . . be it history or legend . . . but one praises more the song of the bard.

Specifications

The Bard's Song Book

24 × 30 feet

Gunite, steel, concrete, earth.

The sculpture will have a steel frame or matrix placed on a concrete footing base or pad. The frame will be sprayed with gunite which will be colored and textured with earth. The earth will be chosen for its color and quality.

Back hoe, concrete mixer, welding torch, gunite dispenser.

No specific maintenance needs.

19) MICHELLE STUART

19B.

19A. Model—earth, plaster, paper, height 4″, width 20″, depth 16¼″
19B. Drawing—pencil, charcoal, graphite, 50 × 58″
Lent courtesy the artist

THE BARD'S SONG BOOK

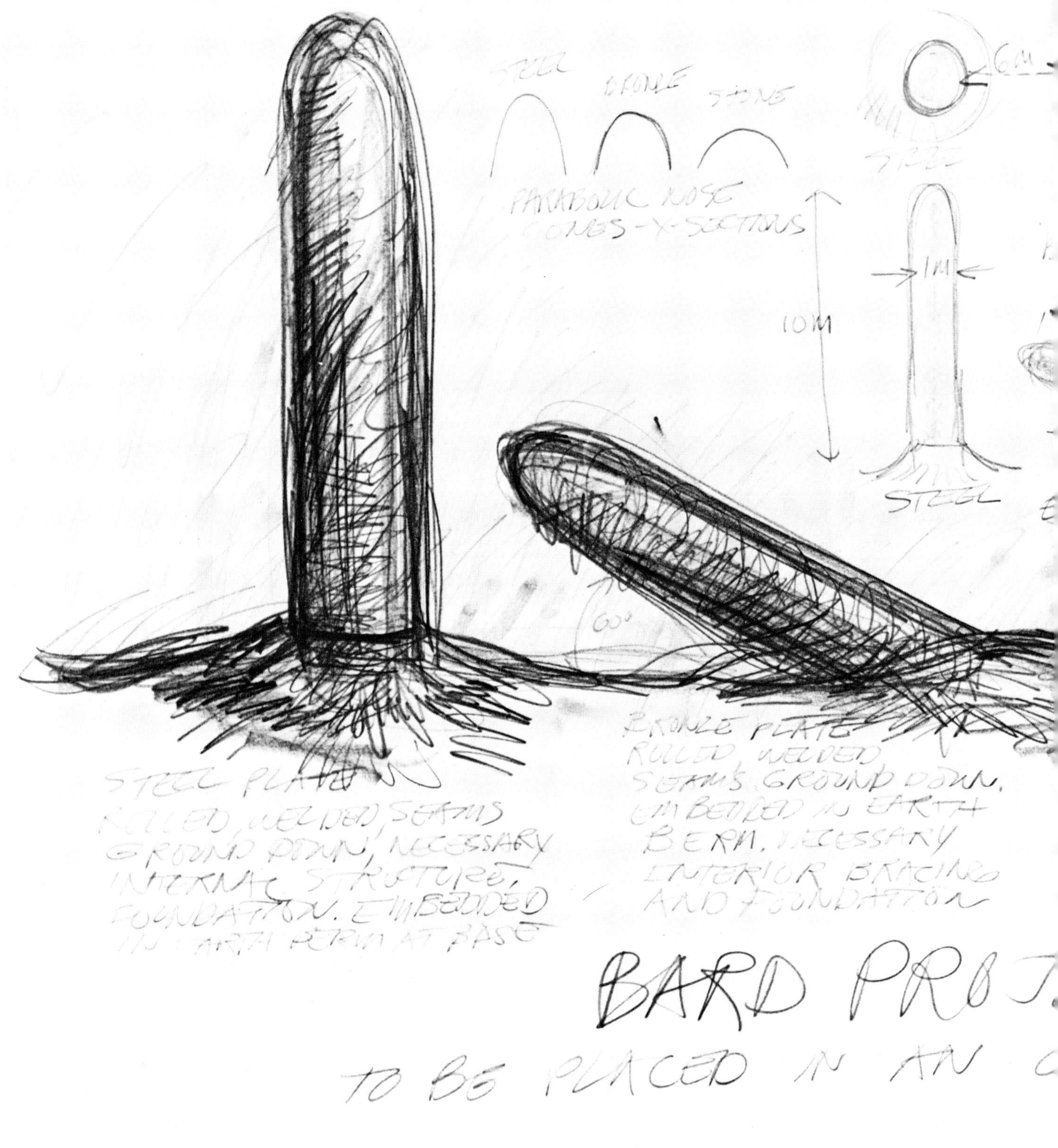

20) ROBERT MORRIS

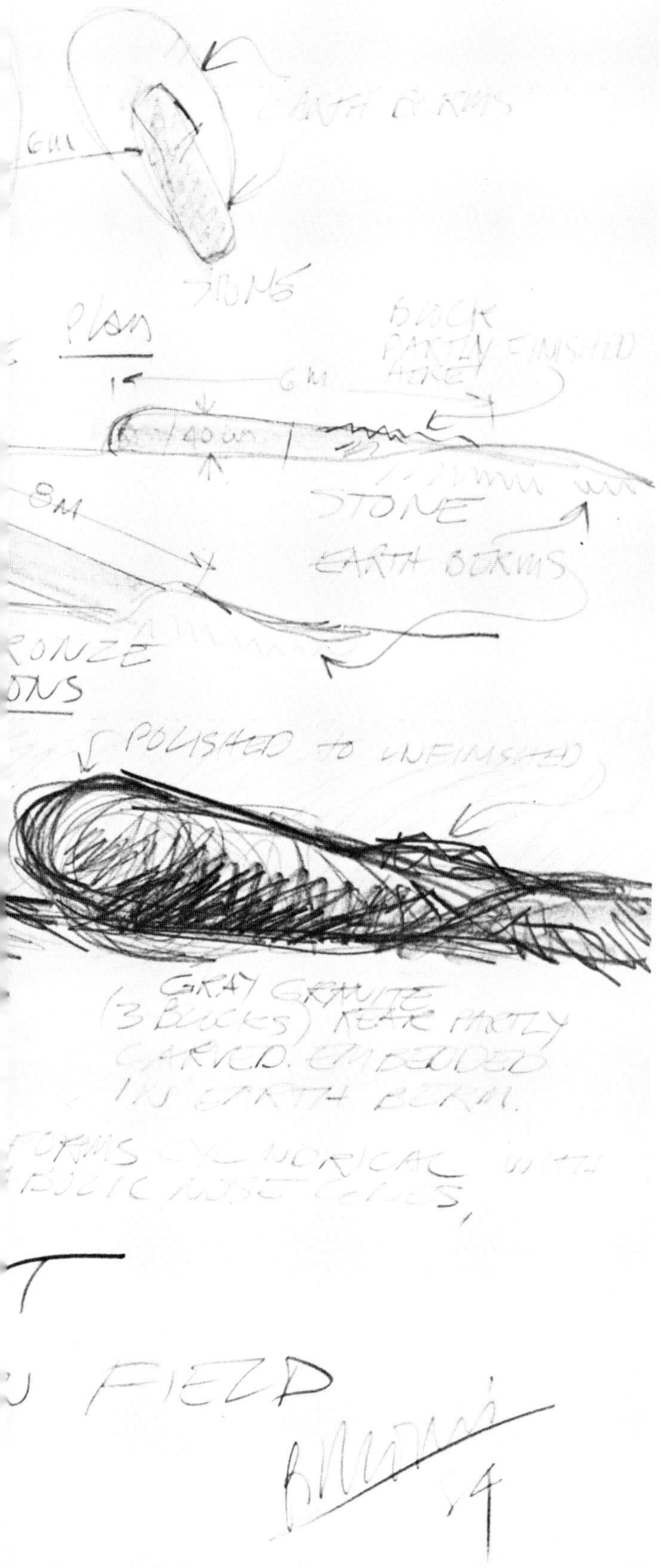

20. Graphite on paper, 38 × 50″
Lent courtesy the artist

UNTITLED

21A.

Artist's statement. This proposal for the **Land Marks** exhibition came out of two sets of facts: the theme of the exhibition—"the relationship between humans, nature and technology"; and my own experiences when I visited the site, a low, almost natural grassy hill, framed by woods and ravines. The particular cues that led to the formal elements were the oak leaves lying on the ground around the site, and the comparable shapes of the ravines on the contour map sent to the participating artists (see collage). I decided to form the hill with agricultural type of terracing (which usually follows the contours of the land) in the general shape of a giant oak leaf, imperceptible as such from ground level. This terracing, planted with grass or ground-cover, would represent the natural element. A number of rectilinear stepped structures of a much smaller scale, interspersed through the hill "at random," would represent the human-made element imposed upon the land. Each of these structures, some of them above ground and some sunken below the terrace levels, is based on one or two rhythmic step patterns (taken from my *Dictionary of Steps,* 1980)—metaphors for modes of thinking. However, their juxtaposition with the more natural terracing was instigated by two earlier experiences: my pondering over the enigmatic sets of steps carved, here and there, on the curvilinear stratified rocky mount across from Sacsayhuaman fortress in Peru (which I visited in 1971); and my fascination with the varied stone fragments imbedded in a common sand medium in the handsome sedimentary rocks of Spetsai, Greece. In my proposal for Bard College, one could perceive the step rhythms as "island universes" of varying structure imbedded in a homogeneous continuum of a different formal nature, interrupting its continuity. Yet, on another realm of scale, one could see the step sequences, at least from an aerial view-point, as caterpillars crawling on the oak leaf, and on an intermediate scale, as human vestiges—marks—left on the stratified land.

To pursue further the theme of the relationship of nature, humans and technology, I have introduced a two-dimensional and conceptual element into the sculpture: blown-up photographs and informational inscriptions, sandblasted (again, imbedded) onto the concrete surfaces of the step sequences, will illustrate major accomplishments of science and technology, and the impending destruction of nature (and humanity) brought on by them. The images and inscriptions will center on the following themes, one per step formation: rocket and space technology, one of the grandest achievements of humankind—and its destructive counterpart, atomic war; great cities with skyscrapers, the most impressive samples of modern building technology—and their infamous results,

(statement continues, p. 53)

21) ATHENA TACHA

21B.

21C.

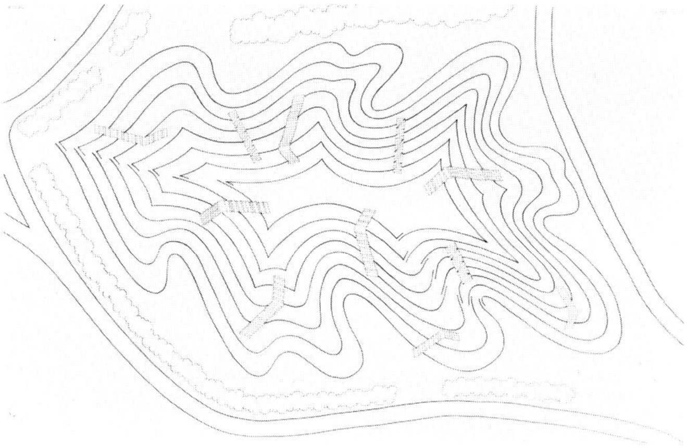

21D.

21A. Model—mixed media, 48 × 30 × 4½″
21B. Model—mixed media, 28 × 28 × 6″
21C. Collage—24½ × 34½″
21D. Drawing—felt tip pens, 31 × 48″
Lent courtesy the artist

LAND MARKS

ARTISTS' STATEMENTS

(Abish, cont. from p. 9)

way, gravel paths, wooded areas, portals, clearance, raised platform and sunken lawn are the augury of events to come.

Entry into the work will lead knowingly or not to the center, the Zone of Absolute Reality.[2]

Materials/Construction:

4′ high cedar deck supported by beams and pressure treated pilings in ground.

6′ × 6″ × 16″ steel reinforced brick walls/4′ deep solid foundation.

3″ perforated tile for drainage/gravel and loose earth fill/copper flashing.

Portals: concrete core with brick facing.

Landscaping: trees, gravel, excavation for 18″ deep sunken lawn.

[1]Friedrich Nietzsche, *The Gay Science* (New York: Random House/Vintage, 1974) 24.
Stoics and Epicureans.—The Epicurean selects the situation, the persons, and even the events that suit his extremely irritable, intellectual constitution; he gives up all others, which means almost everything, because they would be too strong and heavy for him to digest. The Stoic, on the other hand, trains himself to swallow stones and worms, slivers of glass and scorpions without nausea; he wants his stomach to become ultimately indifferent to whatever the accidents of existence might pour into it: he reminds one of that Arabian sect of the Assaua whom one encounters in Algiers: like these insensitive people, he, too, enjoys having an audience when he shows off his insensitivity, while the Epicurean would rather dispense with that, having his "garden"! For those with whom fate attempts improvisations—those who live in violent ages and depend on sudden and mercurial people—Stoicism may indeed be advisable. But anyone who foresees more or less that fate permits him to spin *a long thread* does well to make Epicurean arrangements. That is what all those have always done whose work is of the spirit. For this type it would be the loss of losses to be deprived of their subtle irritability and be awarded in its place a hard Stoic hedgehog skin.

[2]Mircea Eliade, *Cosmos and History* (New York: Harper Torchbooks, 1954) 17.

(Feigenbaum, cont. from p. 12)

way and of the cascading water. The natural wood bridges across the canal openings are intended not only as crossings but as rest spots over the water.

The proposal is presented in the form of a big three-dimensional contour map and is a play on time and place. The spiral terrace is reminiscent of South American terracing and is intended to inspire appreciation of similar cultural forms. The lower right corner of the map is rolled up enough to reveal a relief of George Washington taken from a Peale painting. Washington is symbolic in the imaginary sense of—this is the landscape that might have been. George was a surveyor by training and later a concerned and frustrated farmer. From reading a selection of his letters one becomes aware of the depth of his involvement with cultivation and its problems. The inscription, "Land can be improved in peacetime only," is not a quotation from Washington but an acknowledgement of how he felt. Because it is intended that this exhibition travel I feel that the relief and its message are an important reminder at this time as is the title of the project "An approximate original contour." This quotation comes from the 1977 surface mining and reclamation act which stipulates that damaged land must be returned to its approximate original contour. Though I am not working with damaged land at Bard, the title is intended to stimulate concern for the natural environment in general.

All specifications at this time are preliminary and subject to change. Room must be allowed for altering the concept if while working I discover that I can improve it or if practical and unforeseen problems arise. Some details should for practical reasons wait until such time as the college decides it is interested in implementing the project.

1. Dimensions: The scale of the model is 1/16″ equals 1′. The 5.7 acre field will be terraced in a pyramidal spiral formation to a maximum height of 50′. This will result in a huge ramp with a slope of less than 1%, except at the two entrances where it will be between 1% and 3% and the entrance to the crest which would be about 3%. The height of the terraces will vary from 5′ to 10′ except at the three entrances where they taper to 0. The terrace will angle in at about 1% (or less) from the outer edge to the inner edge. Anyone walking on the spiral will not be aware that they are walking on a sloping surface.

Approximately 7 acres of ravine would be terraced to create a park around the skating rink. These terraces would be level and generally about 10′ high. The protective wall or cliff around the rink would vary from 10′ to 16′ high depending on where recreation and ice clearing facilities are located. (see description)

The dimensions of the rink are: length 564′ by width 168′ at the widest point and 20′ at the narrowest point. The shape of the rink makes it possible to accommodate speed, figure and general skating simultaneously as opposed to a geometrically designed rink. The island in the rink is intended as a rest area.

The canals emanating from the crest of the spiral are two separate waterways. The shorter one flowing west is 240′ long. The flow east into the lake is 604′. The canal walls will vary to a maximum height of 10′ and in keeping with the terraces at specific points.

The pine trees (possibly Norway Spruce) in the terraced ravine are indicated on the model as approaching the maximum potential height for this species of over 100′. The Norway Spruces along the roadway are being shown at the same height for consistency. The dimensions of the natural wood bridges over the canals would vary in length from about 30′ to about 50′.

2. Materials: The spiral pyramid would be constructed of fill with a high percentage of stone. All the terracing is to be stone faced and a variety of plants, vines and grasses, will prevent erosion of the terrace walls. The spiral terraces would be planted in perennial grasses and clover plus flowers. Along the banks of the waterways it would be desirable to try such flowering plants as columbine which blooms from April to July and is easy to cultivate, rose mallow which does well in mud, and if possible the cardinal flower which does well near moving and still waters and is on the protection list because of over picking.

In the terraced ravine many of the existing plants would be saved especially trees in esthetically strategic locations. Ground cover would include most of the varieties natural to that spot (growing there now) plus other varieties.

Configurations of natural stone would be added to the waterways for esthetic purposes. I would expect the water beds, both canals and lake to be stone and would not anticipate using concrete anywhere.

The natural wood crossings would be Cedar or Douglas Fir depending on availability. Sections fixed into the ground would be treated with wood life and need not be replaced more frequently than every 50 years or so.

3. Method of construction: Terracing would obviously be accomplished with earth moving equipment exclusively. Though not indicated on the model at this time a network of stone steps (natural rough stone) would lead into the ravine to the rink. This would require some hand work, but not much. Planting on the terraces would be done in large part by machine with some hand planting. Drains are to be built where the canals terminate. These will be of natural stone. A run-off system, essentially several tunnels, would be built into the lake wall at strategic points to ensure that the water level does not rise too high, though this is hardly likely given the limited water source.

Labor and machine requirements: As indicated above the majority of the project would be accomplished with earth moving and general construction equipment. This kind of job should be awarded through a system of bidding and with a definite time frame in mind. The project realistically would take a couple of years to realize. Several types of contractors would be involved. A hydraulics engineer would have to be consulted with regard to the water works and their drainage systems as would the grounds personnel at Bard when it came time to make decisions about specific plant species.

Maintenance needs: I expect to select plants that would require little or no maintenance at all. I do not anticipate mowing anywhere for instance. Terrace walls should be checked after every winter season and water beds cleared of debris. It would be highly desirable to build an enclosure to house ice clearing equipment near the rink (also built into the terrace wall). This would permit the college to use the rink to maximum advantage. The ice would need to be cleared of bumps initially, then only after it snows.

(Oppenheim, cont. from p. 21)

Method of construction: armature placed on concrete footing on site, materials pre-cut and pre-rolled, welded on site to armature, primer coat and finish coat of enamel and fiberglass labor and machine requirements: factory to prepare armatures, to cut and roll rigid materials to an approximate diameter, weld steel rod to armatures, pour foundations, set structure, wrap armature using come-alongs and other devices, weld on site, finish surfaces.

Maintenance: possible re-painting when necessary.

Site: in an open area with tall grass, such as site #3.

Roots in Cubism. Hearts in the Stars. (Forest for Cezanne)

The objective of this work is to bring to the physical setting of the campus a rich and historical art event that occurred within the world of illusion. This work interprets Cezanne's "discovery" of Cubism as having occurred by looking at trees and seeing the geometric structures within them. The work incorporates metal arcs to indicate comet trails from celestial origins.

Dimensions: 14′ × 8′ in diameter

Materials: marine plywood, tinted and stained, ½″ mild steel plate, rolled to a conic 8.5′ ring, pre-cut boulder, cement foundation, 4.5′ diameter tree trunk.

Method of construction: fabricate top portion of tree using a steel rod armature, bores holes into pre-cut wood shapes, attach to armature and to each other (tongue and groove method), stain with a colored wood preservative, place trunk on site over a poured concrete foundation, attach top to trunk, place boulder and steel arc.

Labor and machine requirements: factory to roll conic ring, landscape personnel to acquire and cut tree trunk and boulder, wood shop to fabricate top section, cement truck to pour concrete, fork lift to place elements.

Maintenance needs: rust-preventive primer applied to steel arc, annual re-application of wood stain for top section.

Site: Ideally, this work would be placed in a dense area of trees, where the scale would be adjusted to scale of the natural trees. Site #5 or #12 seems to fit this requirement.

(Perry, cont. from p. 24)

for construction of this work; Ferric nitrate, muriatic acids and other chemical compounds will be necessary to obtain the desired surfaces.

Once the weathering of the corten has ripened the surface to a dark eggplant brown, it should be wire brushed and rubbed down with a 50/50 solution of linseed oil and turpentine once a year. No other maintenance is necessary.

The artist will be involved physically with this sculpture from start to finish. A small model will not be given to a fabricator to "blow up" to size. Large sculptures demand delicate adjustments in reference to the relationships of the parts to the whole, as well as to the surrounding environment which must be responded to constantly by the artist as the work develops.

This sculpture, (TRANS-12), not only incorporates a response to the changes in the season, but the seasons as part of the total environment will play a part in the evolution of this piece, from structural considerations such as choice of material to design factors such as prevailing winds, wind velocities, ground heave caused by freeze and thaw, rain, snow, etc.

The contour of the terrain and the surrounding trees and buildings determined the sizes and shapes of the elements of the sculpture and their relationship to each other and their placement. The immediate environment dictated the scale and the way the parts of the sculpture move in and with the landscape and with each other. The greater environment, which includes one's awareness of the river and the mountains, was also a factor in determining scale, material, color, and force. (By force, I am referring to the awesome tension that can be created by the juxtaposition of forms.)

In order not to be overwhelmed by the space of the open field, the trees, the sky, and the brooding over-hang that the river and mountains hold in the unconscious, this work has to have a commensurate grandeur of scale. Size alone will not do this. Each element in the structure must relate to the rest of the piece and to the place around it in such a way as to build up visual tension. The illusion of great volume is created by playing angle against space, rough edge against smooth, thus the abstract idea of volume and force is implied. The rough edges and the shapes of the steel elements may seem to suggest an anthropomorphic allusion, however, actually this technique is used to set up a "vibration" of visual rhythm of tree, cloud, field and mountain.

The forms of this sculpture will rise from the ground as though thrust up by some antedeluvian event. They will be securely anchored to cement and reinforcing rod footings.

Elements of steel come from the earth and the molecules expand, contract, change color and move with changes in temperature. It is a 'living' material, subject to changes in the environment, and these are considerations in this work. In addition, the material is appropriate for this work because it is strong and needs little maintenance, and the natural colors are appropriate for a large outdoor sculpture in this site—enabling it to participate in the landscape rather than impose itself upon it. The dull finish stainless steel reflects colors in the environment—blue sky, green leaves, autumn leaf colors,—and tho' this dull stainless steel is strangely white in snow, it also reflects deep purple and blue shadows. The corten, being a dark purple brown, casts a lavender light on the stainless steel. The colors and textures seem to change endlessly, but always in accord with the environment, reflecting, enhancing and going with that which surrounds it.

(Pinto, cont. from p. 34)

Construction: Running concrete channel foundation 24″ deep for entire structure. Block to be mortared and spaced to allow for seeding between blocks. Angle irons to run from poured concrete form in center of wheel to outer wall of wheel. Cut timber for roof to be laid inside angle iron.

Labor and machine: Crew of 4, cement mixer, welding equipment, generator cherry picker or lift.

Maintenance: Seeding and watering first few weeks, then nothing.

Speaking in Tongues Project Series: *Tower for the Study of Languages*

The First Tool
Articulate Vocal Sound

Split Tongue
Stutter
Tongues of Fire
Loss of Speech
Speech—"The capacity that defines us as sovereign over nature"

Dimensions: 45′H, 10′ at base. Angle iron entrance: 7′H × 3′W.

Materials: Timber, concrete, angle iron, seed, cable hoist, and chair.

Construction: Concrete foundation 6′ deep.

Labor and Machine: Crew of 4, cement mixer, welding equipment, generator.

Maintenance: Seeding and watering first few weeks, then nothing.

(Tacha, cont. from p. 48)

endless refuse and pollution of the landscape; fast means of communication with their accessories, such as handsome bridges and superhigways—and their inevitable handicaps, such as air and noise pollution, traffic jams, junk yards and depletion of natural resources; highly sophisticated industry—and its lamentable after-effects, air and water pollution and radioactive wastes; computers, a tremendous extension of the brain—with their threat of possible domination of the human mind; genetic engineering with its curative potential—and its frightening possibilities of biological warfare and human gene manipulation. The partial model, on a four times larger scale than the model for the entire piece, gives an idea of this use of photographic documentation, and the accompanying page presents a sampling of the kind of inscriptions that would be sandblasted on the steps.*

Normal building equipment and expertise will be needed for the construction of the piece: bulldozers for moving the earth for the terraces and brick-layers for building the retaining walls (in stone or brick); reinforced concrete casting crews for the step formations; sandblasting equipment for the images and inscriptions. Care will be taken not to interfere with the water-pipes and telephone cables that cross the land; and drainage will be provided for the sunken sets of steps, all of which have their lowest step at least a couple of feet above ground level. At two or more crucial points, a series of ramps will offer easy accesses to the terraces for the handicapped and lawnmowers, the only equipment needed for maintenance of the work.

Sampling of inscriptions for sunken steps, documenting the theme of *Great Cities*—the achievements of modern building technology, versus environmental pollution:

The Empire State Building in New York City, built in 1931, was the tallest building in the world for nearly half a century, with 102 stories. It was surpassed in 1977 by the World Trade Towers in lower Manhattan, with 110 stories.

The Verrazano-Narrows bridge in New York City, connecting Staten Island to Brooklyn in 1964, became the longest bridge in the world, with 4,260 ft. span and 228 ft. maximum clearance. The longest New York bridge before that was the George Washington bridge, built in 1931, with 3,500 ft. span and 212 ft. clearance.

New York City generates more than 70% of the sewage sludge dumped in the ocean. Wastes, chemicals, dredged spoil, garbage and leacheate from landfills, vessel discharges, and urban runoff add to the water's pollution.

New York City discharges 1.3 billion gallons of waste water into the Hudson River, Jamaica Bay and New York Harbor every day. Twelve New Jersey sewage plants which treat wastes from industry add to the same waters another 600 million gallons of wastewater per day.

The Hudson and East Rivers receive 250 million gallons of *raw* sewage per day.

Urban-produced fine particulate matter in the air can cause a variety of diseases, from cancer and asthma, to eye problems and nervous disorders.

Fine particles are regularly transported by the winds to pollute environments and affect the rain acidity as far as 2,500 kilometers from their source.

Rainfall whose acidity may have increased as much as ten to a hundred times by sulfates and nitrates (from industrial smoke, automobile exhaust, etc.) has serious consequences for forest ecosystems as well as for crops and other vegetation.

Beverage containers are estimated to make up as much as 7% of the total weight of municipal refuse.

Plastic baggies, a non-biodegradable material, have brought near to extinction the giant sea-turtle, who swallows them in mistake for jelly-fish. Plastic bags and beer cans are also the greatest visual pollutants of beaches and recreation areas.

Sampling of inscriptions for raised steps, documenting the theme of *Rocketry*—the achievements of space technology versus nuclear weapons:

On October 4, 1957, Sputnik I, an artificial satellite launched by the U.S.S.R., was the first object to be placed in orbit around the Earth by the human race.

The U.S.A. satellite Apollo II landed the first human being on the Moon, on July 20, 1969.

One of the U.S. Viking satellites landed for the first time on another planet, Mars, in July 1976.

The U.S. satellites Voyager I and II explored photographically the outer planets Jupiter and Saturn between 1979 and 1981.

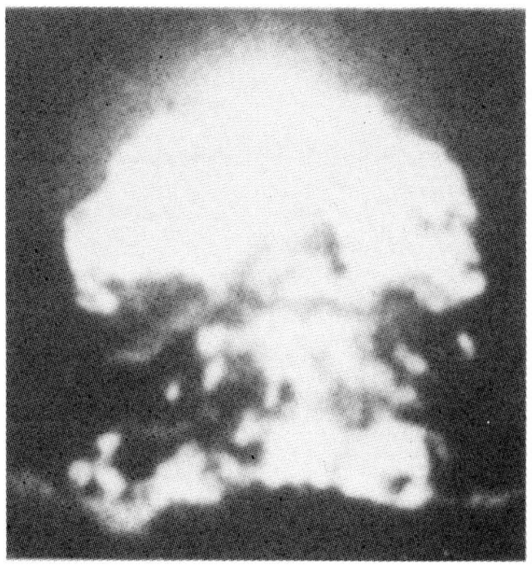

In 1982, the U.S.A. and the Soviet Union together had some 50,000 nuclear warheads, 16,000 of which were strategical intercontinental bombs and missiles. One of them would kill two million people.

A modern 15 megaton nuclear bomb is equivalent to 1,200 Hiroshima explosions happening simultaneously.

In the seconds following the detonation, an atomic bomb would create a huge fireball with temperatures of 20 to 30 million degrees Fahrenheit. Anyone even glancing at the fireball from as far away as 35 miles would be blinded by retinal burning.

The shock wave created by a nuclear explosion would cause skull fractures, ruptured lungs, broken backs and massive hemorrhages. Even a dozen miles from the center of the explosion, the overpressure would explode windows, hurling their glass fragments at a hundred miles per hour.

After a nuclear explosion, spontaneously started fires, fueled by gasoline stations, gas lines, oil storage tanks, would transform a whole city into a firestorm with temperatures as high as 1,600° Fahrenheit. People in shelters would be roasted as in a crematorium, if not asphyxiated as the fire would suck oxygen out of their shelters.

*Nonetheless, even in the scale of the partial model (¼ in.=1 ft.), the images still have to be proportionately larger than they would be in reality in order to be at all distinguishable; therefore, their positioning cannot be definitive, and there are fewer of them. Moreover, in reality the photographic images would merge much more with the architectural surfaces, as they would be lightly incised into them (not applied) and be almost the same color (not black and white).

Four Discussions of the Land Marks Projects

Art Historians: Lawrence Alloway and Shelley Rice

Ecologists: Erik Kiviat and Daniel Simberloff

Sculpture, Nature, the Environment

Lawrence Alloway

Much of the environmental art of the 20th century has been implicitly urban, conceived as an extension of architecture, not like Michael Singer's primitive hut in the present show, but mass-produced modular architecture. This is true of art and architecture complexes, such as the University of Caracas, where works by Calder, Vasarely, and others are abundant, and of single pieces, such as Claes Oldenburg's "Batcolumn," 1977, in Chicago. The rehabilitation of the idea of public sculpture in the United States reinforces this urbanistic base certainly, since public art assumes a certain density of population if the work is to be truly considered public. Years ago a section of the journal *The Tiger's Eye* was devoted to the theme, "Ivy on the Doric Column."[1] This evocative phrase neatly summarizes the contrast of geometry and forms of growth, not simply as time's passage spoiling the marble, but as a return to the realm of nature.

The artists in **Land Marks** define nature in a variety of ways, but their preoccupation with it is undeniable. The approach of sculpture to nature is rarely the route of representation, which works well with figures as objects, but not with scenic space: scenic sculpture of landscape tends to produce theatrical imagery, like stage sets.[2] The artists here tend to occupy the landscape itself, either by shaping it (earthworks) or by construction that incorporates aspects of the natural context. Cecile Abish's "Epicurean Arrangements," for example, proposes a processional form in which a deck is approached via arches and the approach is part of the sculpture. When the participant boards the deck and turns around, the whole space, as it were, will be given back, newly seen and from another angle. Jackie Ferrara also proposes a deck-piece, but it lacks the ironies of Abish and seems dominated by the sense of being a place for performance. Nancy Holt's "O Silo," a cluster of towers and domes, is perforated according to the sun's position at the summer and winter solstice, which sets the specific site into a solar schedule. Processional movement and solar coordinates both posit the site as the vital starting point. Charles Ross's "When the Stars Speak Shape" proposes a massive symmetrical presence on site, but like an observatory it will be minutely calibrated to celestial north with a functioning internal chamber that admits "a crescent of light."

Time is essential to all these sculptures: it is, so to say, the gift of nature to art (the ivy on the doric column). Sculpture is customarily defined in connection with time, compared to the singular, all-at-once presence of painting, but time is especially acute in nature-based sculpture. The interpenetration of the temporal and the spatial takes various forms, including spectator mobility (Abish, Tacha), time as a planetary or stellar system (Holt, Ross), seasonal change (Sonfist's tower of fallen leaves), and cultural time (Singer's primal house). Paths, calibration, nature-materialism, primitivism, all provide means for activating different faces of our sense of time.

What has happened is that the relation of sculpture to nature turns out to be unexpectedly flexible and sophisticated, far beyond our expectations of a simple nature-romanticism. The games with systems of Conceptual art are, unexpectedly, highly appropriate for use in landscape, amplifying and extending a given site without dulling the sense of place or losing a sense of real materials. Conceptual art in its original documentary form reached an early point of exhaustion, but as this exhibition shows, it persists as a play with order in such environmental work as Ross's and Denes's. Denes's "Pascal's Triangle—System of Logic/Logic of Systems" turns diagrammatic form into a visually engaging web of steel cables. Conceptual art benefits from a renewed sense of art as object and at the same time confers complexity of site-specific work.

Linda Weintraub's title for this exhibition is witty and accurate. The word *landmark* has three senses: 1. "prominent or conspicuous object. . . that serves as a guide. . . to travellers"; 2. "a prominent or distinguishing feature, part, event"; and 3. "something used to mark the boundary of land" *(Random House Dictionary,* unabridged). The first usage, as a sign of place or positional indicator, is richly explored in the projects. The second sense (of a notable site) may become appropriate when one of the projects is realized at full scale on the Bard campus. The third sense emphasizes the landmark as a sign, a human artifact. Environmental art is rarely abstract, both because of its interaction with the site (and hence with the spectators or participants) and because of the ways in which nature is incorporated into the art.

The artists in this exhibition are largely ambiance-responsive in a way different from the outdoor sculpture of, say, Marino Marini, Henry Moore, and David Smith with their working assumption of self-contained but mobile sculptures that can be parked anywhere. (Mobile, that is, not in the sense of possessing moving parts, but being themselves movable as whole sculptures). The dominant impetus towards an art that incorporated the environment as structural and contentual factors was provided by the early earthworks, 1968-1973. These include Michael Heizer's "9 Nevada Depressions," 1968, and "Double Negative," 1969, which is also the

Alan Sonfist, "Time Landscape," 1965.

year of Walter de Maria's "Las Vegas Piece." In 1970 Robert Smithson's "Spiral Jetty" was carried out into the Great Salt Lake, though it should be remembered that Smithson's theory and practice of Sites/Non-Sites preceded all the earthworks. His speculative and revisionary ideas revivified nature as a subject for artists in the late '60s.[3] Smithson's "Spiral Hill" and "Broken Circle," 1971, belong chronologically with the first group of earthworks, but the precisely shaped forms and accessible location anticipate later site-specific sculpture.

The earthworks are large in scale and on remote sites, partly because real estate is affordable in the desert, partly because the journey (pilgrimage) and solitude of the site are part of the meaning. These early works are literally environmental: you trudge along the dead-straight mile-long, bull-dozed swipe of "Las Vegas Piece," slide down into the great notch of "Double Negative" and look across the canyon to the matching cut, or hobble along the rubble-strewn route of "The Spiral Jetty," or did before the lake rose to cover it. The only materials used are constituents of the given site. The second generation of earthworkers usually drop difficulty of access as an esthetic factor and make art of an average sociability. In addition most artists use imported materials (from architectural construction or the fine arts); the scale is often intimate, the forms intricate. Such sculptures are no longer site-specific on a material basis, but they are constructed according to a variety of site-derived cues and references.

The earthworks in Nevada, Utah, and Texas are in out-of-the-way places which is part of their meaning: remoteness protects the sites' solitude.[4] Later, site-specific sculpture is called back from the pilgrimage route to art's regular channels, to parks, museum grounds, and as here the campus. A campus is well suited to works like these in the **Land Marks** exhibition which have their origin in the artists' personal preoccupations but are oriented towards real-space. A campus is a social space, neither concentrated on an audience pre-selected for its interest in art nor on an unsorted general public. The campus is a zone between protected viewing (museum) and random exposure (the street).

By placing earthworks at the head of my short-term view of environmental sculpture I am suggesting that it is crucial to what followed. However, I don't want to appear to reduce matters too much by consigning the artists to a second generation of earthworks. The fact that I believe Conceptual art has been assimilated by some of the artists should warn against over-simplification. However, if we assume that pro-nature, site-specific practices are common to both generations, it makes historical sense of the move from big-scale, heroic projects to smaller-scale intricate ones. Also it blunts criticism of the first generation for anti-ecological procedure and a rough pragmatism in their bull-dozing or blasting.[5] The work which we face here is intricate, intimate, subtle, a highly developed art which requires an earlier establishing phase for its ideas.

Kate Linker has pointed out that for some contemporary sculptors site is not a pure concept but may denote "a generalized space, whether clearing or glade, forest or field"[6] to which existing ideas are adapted by scale-changes. It is a sharp observation and one supported by the scale of a work that may be in the background of the later generation's work, Alberto Giacometti's "The Palace at 4:00 AM," 1932-33. It is a small work, a table sculpture, but the environment is present in sign form if not as occupiable space. It is an image of dreams of course (4:00 AM) and the subjectivity of its schematic forms is amenable to later symbolism. However, later environmental sculpture tends to offer habitable space at the scale of the world to the viewer or participant which is one reason for insisting on the influence of earthworks. Play sculpture as it developed into a kind of landscape is to be allowed for as a predisposing factor. It shows perhaps in a sculpture like Athena Tacha's, with its ascending and descending flights of steps. The participatory space, the multiplicity of levels, the game of circulation, though conducted with all Tacha's grace has its analogue in the playground.

Reflections on the proposals: it is true I am writing about works on paper, but I am extrapolating them to the projected sites. The exhibition exists on paper and in model form, but the artists have been marvelously explicit in detail and clear in their visualizations. Therefore what I am talking about may not be too far from their intentions. One of the stands of formalist criticism was that intention was irrelevant to art: only the outcome rated; the product was the sole legitimate subject. I prefer to follow the lead of the exhibition, a show of intentions, and discuss the sketches as preliminary realities. The form of the show is essentially a mix of architectural presentation drawings (designed to aid client visualization) and Conceptual art (a show of documents).

The land available to the artists at Bard College consists of an open field in front of the Blum Art Institute itself, a rounded sloping triangular green, surrounded by a wooded ravine. A majority of the artists selected the field, with

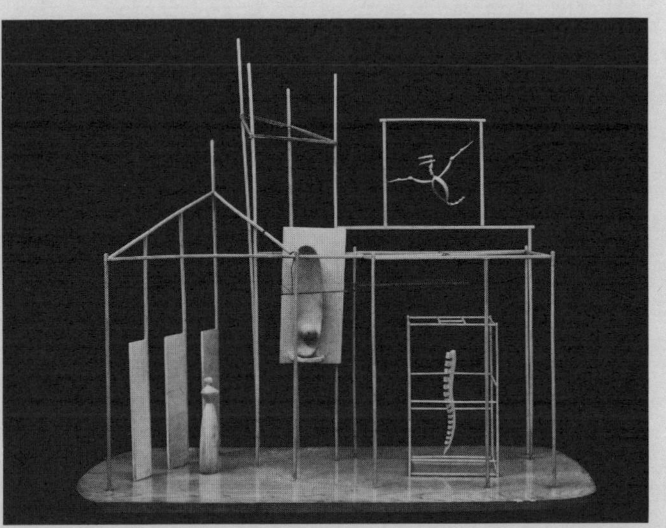

Giacometti, Alberto. "The Palace at 4:00 AM," 1932-33. Wood, wire, glass, string, 25×28¼×15¾″. Collection, The Museum of Modern Art, New York.

its maximum visibility, but two opted for the steep woods, Sonfist with his tower of leaves, and Carolee Thea with her Daphne project: she proposes six sculptures of a running figure, distributed through the trees like a three-dimensional Muybridge motion study, as the woman flees rape by Apollo. The most comprehensive program for the field is Harriet Feigenbaum's work with the deceptively modest title, "An Approximate Original Contour," in which she would terrace the area and introduce "a network of stepped canals" culminating in a winter skating rink. She carries sculpture into the realm of landscape gardening which has the effect of not only expanding the definition of sculpture but of confounding the boundaries of fine art and craft. This means the acceptance of seasonal change, absorbing it into the work itself, but also a relaxation of the traditional idea of art as the setting of formal limits, boundaries that assure esthetic identity. The soft-edged works in the show, such as Feigenbaum's and Sonfist's, postulate a form of art free of compactness, the last tyranny of formalist esthetics.

It has been suggested that women have a natural affinity for the earth, despite the absence of women from the first generation of earthworks and despite the fact that most women in the second generation share their attitudes and styles with male artists. The increased presence of women among the sculptors is notable, but not necessarily to be explained by an affinity of womb and earth. One artist in the present show who does affirm the link to the earth is Ana Mendieta. Her proposal for an effigy to be dug in the field presents a female presence expanding outward from her center. By chance the rudimentary image of a woman as "a hole in the ground" complements a male simplification in Robert Morris's proposal. This consists of three identical cylinders, of steel, bronze, and grey granite, the latter partly buried and horizontal, the second at an angle of 60 degrees, and the first upright. The sequence implies erection of course, but the different materials give a touch of opulence to the cliché. Jody Pinto's "Five Spoke Catherine Wheel" expands like a five-legged spider, giving her proposed sculpture a dark creatural undertone. With the added tower thrusting up from the center of the wheel, a second directional force is abruptly added. In "Tower for the Study of Languages," a separate proposal, there is a strong phallic potential in the shaft. These works are of course stable but the first carries plants and the second is designed for entry. Such elements preserve the environmental base of both works, despite their substantial bulk and animated profiles.

There is one sculpture about which I feel reservations in the context of **Land Marks**, Beatrice Perry's "Trans-12." It would not be fabricated on the site and is essentially a mobile sculpture adjustable to the conditions of different sites although based on the tree-line of this specific site. The nine free-standing units, of corten and stainless steel, are even made of the stand-by materials of international multi-service sculpture.

Michael Singer's architectural space touches on the pre-industrial imagination common to many nature-oriented artists. His hut, containing clear demarcations between different burial (sleep?) areas, suggests ethnic architecture, the visual equivalent of the ethno-poetics of Jerome Rothenberg. Orderly placement seems to evoke the belief pattern of another culture. Michelle Stuart's proposal of a vast open book to be called "The Bard's Song Book" alludes to the college and to Shakespeare, but the huge earthen pages imply a greater antiquity, a precedent age of giants. Robert Stackhouse's sculpture is "related to ships: abandoned, wrecked, a graveyard of Hudson River history," but again there is the suggestion of more ancient precedent, in this case, Viking burial ships. Helen and Newton Harrison's "Pure Water Still" is, however, thoroughly contemporary in its use of solar technology. From a functional barn-like building on the field above the Blum Art Institute distilled water would flow downhill to an outlet in the gallery. Is this perhaps the first example of eco-Dada?

The triple spheres representing schemata of the world in Alice Aycock's "A Refutation of the Second World" show that she has moved from her extrapolations of Vladimir Tatlin's "Monument to the Third Republic," 1919-20, to a kind of global imagery. In their grandeur and arbitrariness, the spheres seem like the model for a brilliant science fiction story. Dennis Oppenheim's sculptures have a tough carnival energy. Unlike most of the artists in **Land Marks** he works less from a sense of the site than against the site. This has been the traditional role of sculpture out-of-doors: rusty against clean forms, rounded volumes against right-angled modules, dark bronze against shiny glass. Oppenheim's sculptures, some of them with tangled art historical references, would pit their fragmented polychrome against the landscape-cycle. This marks a climax of the esthetics of contrast in which sculpture is everything—the context, the site, is not.

Linda Weintraub has brought two professions together for this catalogue, ecology and art criticism. I have read with pleasure articles by Erik Kiviat and Daniel S. Simberloff, though not the ones for this occasion. My impression is of Kiviat as an empirical observer of animal behavior, which he tracks assiduously and analyzes; Simberloff is a student of evolutionary form by statistical methods. One man uses waders, the other a computer. What is the connection of ecology and art? I doubt that art can function humanely in ecological terms, if we are thinking of direct intervention into animal or plant communities. However, as society's awareness of interrelationships in the ecosphere has been consolidated since, say, the first Earth Day in 1970, it should be an optimistic measure of natural complexity. Ecology is not merely the index of pollution, though it includes that, it is awareness of the interaction of multiple, overlapping life-forms.

---

[1] "Ivy on the Doric Column." *The Tiger's Eye,* 3. Greenwich, Conn., 1948.

[2] Hillwood Art Gallery, Long Island University, 1984. "Reflections: New Conceptions of Nature." Curated by Judith K. Collischan Van Wagner.

[3] *The Writings of Robert Smithson.* Edited by Nancy Holt. New York, 1979.

[4] See "Site Inspection," in the author's *Network: Art and the Complex Present,* pp. 247-254, Ann Arbor, 1984.

[5] Hostility towards Smithson for muddled "ecological" reasons is implicit in several articles in *Art In the Land,* Edited by Alan Sonfist. New York, 1983.

[6] Kate Linker, "Michael Singer: A Position In, and On, Nature." *Art In the Land*, p. 184.

Landmarks and Landscape: The Ecology of Site Works

Erik Kiviat

Introduction

There is a place where grasses cover clay soil, in a patchwork of fields separated by wooded ravines, halfway from the knoll at the core of Bard College to the steep bluffs fronting on a bay of the Hudson River. Here the tides undulate through fresh water, deep and shallow, filling and draining the marshes bordered by the shell debris from millenia of Indian encampments, and the Eurasian plants from the 19th-century lords of the manor. It is my aim in this essay to consider, from an ecologist's point of view, the Bard College site, the proposed artworks, and the role of large-scale outdoor art in the landscape, and in human culture.

Natural History of the Site

The regional setting is dominated by the Hudson River. Tidal for 150 miles from Manhattan to the dam at Troy, it is an avenue for weather, smog, commercial shipping, pleasure boating, and migrating fish and birds. The Hudson's sunsets and storms are magnificent. At Bard, the river is strictly freshwater though experiencing a four-foot rise and fall of the tides twice daily. South Bay (Fig. 1) is reduced to a sheet of water and mudflats at low tide, but just off Cruger Island the river is 60 feet deep. The Tivoli South and North Bays comprise one of the largest and richest freshwater-tidal wetlands on the Hudson. The bulk of the bays and portions of the surrounding uplands are a State Unique Area, an Experimental Ecological Reserve, and one of four sites in the Hudson River Estuarine Sanctuary. Where the Saw Kill, the stream that forms the southern boundary of the Bard College lands, flows into South Bay is the Bard College Ecology Field Station. The entire east bank of the Hudson for about a mile inland, and stretching several miles north and south of the college, is a State Scenic Area and a National Historic District.

Inland from the river on both shores, the land rises in a stepwise fashion, the climate becomes cooler, and the countryside more sparsely populated. The changes are more striking on the west shore which lies at the foot of the Catskill Mountains.

The bedrock underneath Bard College is gray sandstone and gray shale, in alternating layers, and is approximately 450 million years old. Outcrops occur in the woods north and south of the main campus knoll, in the bed of the Saw Kill, and in a few places along the edges of the bays of the Hudson River (Fig. 1). The sandstone is stronger and usually "supports" the topographic high points such as ridges, waterfalls, and the headlands projecting into South Bay. When the most recent glaciers melted about 8,000 years ago, sediments of clay and silt, and deposits of sand were formed in a vast lake where ice and debris had dammed a large portion of the Hudson. Elsewhere, there remained "glacial till," a mixture of clay, rocks, and intermediate-sized particles. Till dominates the landscape approximately east of Annandale Road. The "Whaleback" (Fig. 1), a north-south oriented symmetrical hill east of the main Rt. 9G entrance to the college, is an excellence example of a drumlin formed beneath the advancing glacial ice.

West of Annandale Road, today's soils formed on the glacial lake clays. These clays are said to be "varved" or composed of thin alternating layers of clay and fine silt laid down in the lake in winter and summer, respectively. When the subsoil is exposed by excavation, the varves are clearly visible as fine-scale banding. The soils are limy and very dense; water does not infiltrate readily. On level areas (including the **Land Marks** field), rainwater collects in pools and puddles where it may stand for days or weeks. On the steep slopes along South Bay and in the ravines around the site, water runs off quickly. These slopes erode readily, especially where the leaf litter and vegetation have been disturbed, and the clays also tend to slump and slide during heavy rains. Small clay slumps have visibly distorted an old carriage road that runs across the ravine wall just north of the field; and west of Blithewood dormitory, a 70-foot wide disk of clay suddenly slid into South Bay during a severe storm in 1976. Much of the lawn northwest of Blithewood rests on a fine sandy soil, attractive to burrowing animals such as woodchucks and moles.

The field itself varies in elevation from 121 to 139 feet above sea level (i.e., above the Hudson River), with the highest point in the northeast. The ravine bottoms to the west, north and east are at elevations of about 40 to 75 feet. Small streams wind through the ravines, heading north and northwest and eventually emptying into South Bay (Fig. 1). These streams, in clay beds, flow intermittently in gullies in their upper reaches, and perenially or nearly so lower down. A miniature floodplain borders the lower reaches.

The vegetation of the field, mowed short in 1984, comprises grasses and forbs (broad-leaved herbs). Among the prominent grasses are little bluestem *(Andropogon scoparius)*, which stands russet in fall and winter, and sweet vernal grass *(Anthoxanthum odoratum),* the first grass to flower in spring. Among the forbs are plantains

Figure 1. Portion of US Geological Survey, 7.5 minute topographic map sheet, Saugerties, N.Y., 1963, showing the vicinity of Bard College. **Land Marks** site is southwest of the word "Athletic" (Avery Art Center not shown). The tidal Hudson River and the Tivoli North and South Bays occupy the left half of the figure; steep-sided ravines in the clays show just east of the bays.

Figure 2. Aerial photograph (March 1980) of the site and surroundings, from Dutchess County Department of Real Property Tax. Buildings of the Bard College main campus at right, and edge of South Bay at left. Conifers (pine, hemlock, spruce) bordering the white **Land Marks** field show as solid dark tone compared to leafless deciduous trees. Art Center is shown.

(Plantago major and *Plantago* sp.), pussytoes *(Antennaria* sp.), bird's-foot trefoil *(Lotus corniculatus),* clovers *(Trifolium* spp.), and ox-eye daisy *(Chrysanthemum leucanthemum).* There are a number of "fairy rings" in the field. These are full or partial circles up to several feet across which show a conspicuous difference in tone or texture of vegetation. Fairy rings are usually the result of a fungus colony that spreads outward in a radial fashion, dying off in the center, and affecting the species or appearance of herbs inside and outside the circle. The fairy rings on the site are probably the result of the fairy ring mushroom *(Marasmius oreades).*

The margins of the field support a variety of planted and spontaneous trees, as well as spontaneous shrubs and herbs. An exceptionally beautiful double row of large white pines *(Pinus strobus)* borders the sides of Blithewood Road on the south edge of the field. These pines, presumably planted in the 1800s in conjunction with landscaping at Blithewood, are 2-3 feet in diameter-at-breast-height (dbh) and about 50-70 feet tall. Some of them have massive branches low on the trunk. Just north of the pines is a straggling row of 6-8 inch dbh red oaks *(Quercus borealis)* planted around 1970. Old, planted Norway spruces *(Picea abies)* border the field on the west, with a few red maples *(Acer rubrum).* Under these trees is a strip of less-often mowed grass with black-eyed susan *(Rudbeckia hirta),* goldenrod *(Solidago),* bindweed *(Convolvulus),* clover, and grape *(Vitis).*

The north edge of the field has a sparse row of 8-10 inch dbh red maples, elms *(Ulmus),* and white ash *(Fraxinus americana)* separated by a 30-foot wide strip of lawn from a densely-wooded fencerow. Here are white ash, elm, white pine, eastern redcedar *(Juniperus virginiana),* cherry *(Prunus),* the shrubs gray dogwood *(Cornus racemosa)* (abundant), Bell's honeysuckle *(Lonicera* x *bella),* staghorn sumac *(Rhus typhina),* and grape vines. North of the fencerow is a goldenrod-dominated oldfield formerly used as a tree nursery.

The east border is dominated by several large white oaks *(Quercus alba),* with large lower branches that spread over the dirt road at the field edge. Between and under these trees are white pine, flowering dogwood *(Cornus florida),* sugar maple *(Acer saccharum),* white ash, red oak, black oak *Quercus velutina),* European buckthorn *(Rhamnus catharticus),* hop hornbeam *(Ostrya virginica),* cherry, Norway spruce, basswood *(Tilia americana),* hemlock *(Tsuga canadensis),* and poison-ivy *(Rhus radicans)*. Just to the east, in the ravine, is a well-developed forest of hemlock, oaks, white ash, beech *(Fagus grandifolia),* sugar maple, tuliptree *(Liriodendron tulipifera),* flowering dogwood, and hop hornbeam, with witch-hazel *(Hamamelis virginiana)* and spicebush *(Lindera benzoin)* beneath, and on the ground, jack-in-the-pulpit *(Arisaema triphyllum),* wild ginger *(Asarum canadense),* Christmas fern *(Polystichum acrostichoides),* marginal woodfern *(Dryopteris marginalis),* false Solomon's seal *(Smilacina racemosa),* occasional red trillium *(Trillium erectum),* red and white baneberry *(Actaea rubra* and *A. alba),* and grape, poison-ivy and Virginia creeper *(Parthenocissus quinquefolia).* The big trees are 12-18 inches dbh (a few to 24 inches). The slope is steep, and the ground hummocky from repeated slumping of the clay.

The trees and shrubs are in leaf from May to October. Shadbush blooms in the woods in April and flowering dogwood in May. In the marshes, goldenclub is resplendent in May, yellow iris graces the waterways in June, Canada lily hangs lush in the tidal swamps in July, and purple loosestrife and pickerelweed flower in July and August. Goldenrods and asters color the field borders in August and September. The waterways are frozen from about Thanksgiving to February or March.

Land Use History

Intermittently for at least 5,000 years, Indians camped on the islands and the edges of the bays to harvest fish, shellfish, and other foods in the river and marshes. In the 1800s and early 1900s, Livingston family members and their descendents created "country seats" with mansions, intensive landscaping, carriage roads, cattle pastures, and swaths cleared for views of the river. There was even an imitation ruins with imported Mayan statuary placed conspicuously on South Cruger Island. The railroad was built by cut-and-fill along the east edge of the Hudson in 1850, and the partly-isolated bays filled rapidly with muck and aquatic vegetation. During the last several decades, Bard College has united several parcels of estate lands with the original St. Stephen's seminary. Forests have redeveloped upon abandoned cropfields, pastures, and pleasure gardens; immense, spreading, once-ornamental trees, and straggling patches and fringes of introduced plants bear witness to sites of former houses, roads, and gardens. Exotics such as blacklocust, Norway spruce, mezereum, yellowwood, Bell's honeysuckle, banana-vine, periwinkle, daylily, plantain-lily, yellow iris, and others struggle with the native flora for space. The grand white pines of the Blithewood Road spawned wind-spread progeny in eroded fields some distance to the south and north. One or more small impoundments, now drained, lay in the bottom of the ravine. The careless walker can stumble into old root cellars, abandoned sewer settling tanks, and foundation holes become woodland pools. Barbed wire fences bordered cattle lots on the clays, and cobbles and boulders from glacial till were puzzle-pieced together for stone walls farther east. A plot in the north-central portion of the **Land Marks** field was used for an organic garden in 1971, and the oldfield just to the north was a tree nursery not long before—and probably an orchard some time earlier. Bard's old theater stood at the east side of the head of the ravine just east of the **Land Marks** field. About eleven years ago a fire that destroyed the theater also scorched the edge of the forest.

Human hands have (mostly) not lain lightly on the Bard lands, but the power of nature to recreate soil and vegetation has covered scars, reduced the loads of sediment carried by runoff towards the river, and continually changed the appearance of the landscape. In prehistoric New York, Indians camped on the Hudson River's islands, tributary mouths, and wetland margins seasonally, probably moving inland to avoid the cold, wet and windy winter shores. The landlords of the 1800s built their mansions on top of the bluffs, 50-150 feet above the river, and cut lanes through the forest for a river view. At the same time, the shoreline-proper teemed with industry: the railroads, boat landings, brickworks, and ice houses, and there were mills on the tributaries wherever there was enough head to turn a wheel. During the first half of the 20th century, much of the riverbank became wild again, and most development occurred inland along the highways. Now residences and a few industries are being built once again on the shoreline, much to the concern of people who enjoy the scenery and wildness of the river.

Relation of the Pieces to the Site

What characteristics of the site and region are reflected in the artworks? That is, How do the works "encapsulate" the quality or ecology of the site? Stackhouse's "River Bones" embodies qualities of the river, boats, wrecks, water, and ruins. Some of the pieces incorporate flowing water, reflecting the streams in the ravines. (If the site were on the main campus knoll, it would lack this quality of flowing water.) The steep slopes are utilized in certain pieces. The encircling by forest is incorporated into Thea's "Daphne Fleeing," and the ceremonial intimacy of the woods is germane to Singer's creation. Perry's sculpture plays on the skyline and silhouettes of the trees. Several pieces recognize the campus populace by providing a stage, structures to climb onto or into, and water to drink. Holt's "O Silo" appreciates the potential to view the river. Other pieces are more abstract, or at least evoke no unambiguous relationship in my mind.

Works of this scale can have a variety of impacts upon the surroundings resulting from the modification of the structure and appearance of the environment and (often more subtly) the rates and directions of natural processes. Since the Hudson River corridor is a region where people are intensely aware of the mutually-reinforcing esthetic, historic and ecological values of the landscape, it is crucial to ask how the pieces would affect this landscape. Site works intentionally change the visual character of the landscape. In the river corridor, there are two distinct landscapes and thus two components to visual impact: that seen from the land, and that seen from the river. The landscape seen from the river in the Barrytown-to-Tivoli reach is mostly forest, with a few docks, the east shore railroad, a village (Glasco, on the west shore), and scattered larger buildings peering through the trees or in the distance.

Impacts on historic character of the region can also be delineated, and these are closely related to visual impacts. Much of the river-side portions of the Palisades Interstate Park system in Rockland County, New York and adjoining New Jersey was preserved as a reaction to construction of high-rise apartment buildings on top of the river cliffs. The scale of riverside construction is still an issue. Modification of the view from Olana, the preserved estate of the painter Frederick Church, is one of the major reasons why a nuclear power plant was not built across the river at Athens. Nonetheless, it has been argued that the grandeur of the views along the river make buildings of the scale of nukes more appropriate than smaller artifacts.

Projects can also have auditory and olfactory impacts. Cedar wood has a strong odor for years, as do some wood preservatives. Moving parts make noise, and some stationary components ping or rumble when expanding and contracting as outdoor temperature changes.

Most of the materials of the proposed pieces are quite durable. Wooden pieces might last decades, metal pieces the same or more, and stone pieces centuries or millenia. Most of the pieces would require minimal maintenance. Vandalism would likely occur, affecting wood pieces more than stone or metal. Most of the pieces do not involve the use of especially toxic materials, with the exception of the mercury in Aycock's piece. However, some toxicity to plants or animals could result from certain metals in alloys in the other pieces, and from any wood preservatives used in the wooden pieces (copper sulphate, copper naphthenate, "creosote" and PCP are increasingly toxic, approximately in that order).

Projects also affect soil, water, air, vegetation, wildlife, energy and maerials consumption, human behavior, and other aspects of the natural and human environment, and are judged on the balance of the benefits and costs to society. A few of the salient potential impacts of the **Land Marks** pieces on the environment of the site and region are listed in Table 1 on page 66. Under the New York State Environmental Quality Review Act (SEQRA), an Environmental Assessment or Environmental Impact Statement might be required for certain of the more ambitious pieces, to explicitly determine if the environmental benefits and costs of the project would be in the interests of the human community. Additionally, the pieces that modify stream flows (including the creation of artificial streams) or that involve substantial excavation might require special permits from the New York State Department of Environmental Conservation and/or the Town of Red Hook. Pieces that include building-like structures (e.g., Feigenbaum, Holt) might require building permits from the Town.

Landmarks and Landscape

A "landmark" is a recognizable component of the landscape. It is a location on a physical or mental map. There are *natural* landmarks: a lone boulder in a field, a lightning-blasted tree, a grove of tall pines, the junction of two streams. There are also *cultural* (artifactual) landmarks: a blaze on the bark of a tree, a painting on a rock, a pink plaster flamingo, and the World Trade Center. The esthetic acceptability of landmarks depends upon our perceptions of the environment, and the landmark's reality and symbolism. Think of the diverse reactions of different persons to the lightning-struck tree or to graffiti on rocks.

Animals make landmarks as well as humans. We readily recognize the beaver dam and pond, a muskrat lodge, anthill, grouse dustbath, or deer trail. We may, however, overlook subtle guideposts like the cattail spike webbed together for winter shelter by the cattail moth caterpillars, or the musky spot of urine that marks the red fox territory. Animal-created landmarks are utilitarian (or incidental, like the holes eaten by a beetle in a water-lily leaf). Perhaps some animal landmarks have an esthetic function, if there is such a thing in the animal world. A woodrat's cache of shiny objects, or the bower of a bowerbird may be esthetic—of course the bower serves a function in the courtship of the female by the male, and the woodrat's hoard may be only some functional behavior gone awry. At least, animal landmarks can be beautiful to the human eye: I am always thrilled to discover the branched gallery of a bark beetle on the trunk of a dead elm. But landmarks created by humans we judge esthetically whether functional or not.

Human landmarks differ from animal landmarks in another way. Through landmarks, we not only communicate information in the present, but also far into the future; and this information is often enhanced or magnified as our culture evolves. We look upon certain artifacts that have persisted from earlier cultures as typifying the "essence" of those times. For example, the Acropolis, the Aztec pyramids, and the Easter Island statues—large, evocative, and more-or-less mysterious—are artifacts that embody the technology of their period as well as a quality of the people who built them. We are impressed proportional to the durability, size, and prominence of artifacts of the past, and by their mystery—that is, the degree to which they are different from site works being created here and now. That the Easter Islanders erected giant stone heads does not describe the people's diet or sex life, although it certainly makes us aware of a part of their spiritual ways. Long-lived artifactual landmarks can also be undertaken for massive practical purposes, such as distributing water in dry lands, as well as built to impress someone with the power of the builders. Yet many—maybe all—such site works reveal something intimate of the relationship of a culture to its environment.

No less powerful through centuries or millenia are the marks of human actions intended not for esthetic or spiritual reasons but only for practical reasons, or not even intentional at all. The deforestation and desertification of Mediterranean lands by goats and fuel-hungry people is a vast, tragic example. Closer to home are also a great variety of modified natural habitats where people have added or removed various kinds of vegetation, increased or decreased the amount of water present, or done practically anything else imaginable. The carving of the slate, "bluestone," marble, and gravel quarries of the Hudson Valley, the deposition of banks and islands of sandy spoil dredged from the Hudson River's navigation channel, and the cut-and-fill ribbons of the Hudson River railroads are also examples of cultural landmarks. All of these works have their esthetic and ecological bad and good.

Cultural landmarks are ecologically different from natural landmarks. Artifacts are suddenly created in a landscape where the plants and animals are not adapted to such structures and materials. The house rat and house sparrow that have evolved as human companions can prey on, compete with, or spread disease to native wild animals and plants, which may also be weakened by toxic substances and displaced by loss of habitat. Yet humankind would clearly not be what it is—even not be at all—without changing the environment of other organisms.

About 1850, where the east shore railroad passed Bard College, the rails were laid atop a 75-foot wide causeway of fill crossing the Tivoli South and North Bays of the Hudson River. Limestone blocks were stacked in the shallows of the river. Crushed limestone ballast was added on top, and beds of cinder accumulated from the old coal-burning locomotives. Herbs, shrubs and trees grow on the fringes of the fill, cut back by hand, herbicides or bulldozer every few years. Gray catbirds, yellow warblers and song sparrows nest abundantly in this right-of-way vegetation. More than any other factor, the railroad causeways have influenced the edges of the Hudson, accumulating sediment from the tidal waters on the sheltered landward side, and causing the marshes to build outward and upward rapidly. The railroad bridges and culverts where the tidewater fills and drains the marshes are good fishing spots. Many persons experience the richness of the plant and animal life of the marshes from the railroad for the first time. Yet the railroad is also a threat to the marshes, for it is a source of toxic substances, foreign plants that compete with native species, and perhaps too great a reduction in the flushing action of the tides for the marshes' long-term health.

The railroad causeways were intended purely for industry (transportation), but have unintentionally influenced patterns of recreational use of the Hudson and dramatically changed the esthetics and ecology of the shores. At the other end of the continuum of utility is the ornamental garden at Bard's Blithewood (estate now dormitory). The garden was not "utilitarian" in the sense of accomplishing some specific, material task, but certainly serves esthetic, recreational, and spiritual purposes by enhancing the relaxation, pleasure, and reflection of people then and now. While the site works proposed for the Bard field lie more to the esthetic than the utilitarian end of this continuum, there is no particular reason to consider them different phenomena ecologically. Utilitarian and esthetic modifications of the landscape both have environmental impacts.

Most of the **Land Marks** pieces share a largeness of scale, durability, some direct or indirect relationship to the site, a game of manipulation or experimentation with materials, and often humor or fantasy. Beyond these few commonalities, they are as diverse as the living organisms or their potential setting: the earthworm, the woodpecker, the plantain and the pine. The pieces look to the broad river or its intimate tributary, the seclusion of the forest or the unfettered meeting of trees and sky. The materials and geometry run the gamut from the forest's timber to the Art Center's glass and ceramic to imaginations of the heavens. And ecologically, this art treads as gently as a cricket in a meadow or as ponderously as a deer in a vegetable garden. I sense a reaching back and ahead in time, tradition-time or esthetic-time, a meeting of Stonehenge with the laser.

"Why" (in an ecological sense) make art? Whatever other reasons operate simultaneously, art plays a role in the adaptation of a society to its environment (broadly including the artifactual and natural environment). The Lascaux cave-painters depicted animals and people for "luck" in the hunt (i.e., to imbue their thoughts and dreams with the ecological and behavioral qualities of the game). The builders of Stonehenge, and builders of celestial markers around the world were (and are) making maps of the seasons and reaching for the mysteries of the changing relationships of sun, earth, weather, the flowering times of plants, the arrival dates of migrating birds, and the sowing, cultivating, and reaping times of crops. The makers of monuments and temples in the valleys of Mexico, Egypt, and Mesopotamia were struggling to regulate the distribution of waters, the salinity of soils, the winter stores of grains, the abundance of wild fish and game, and the distances to envious and unfriendly tribes.

Larger and more deadly, perhaps, but not too unlike the social and environmental problems faced by these ancient artists, are the social-ecological threats of 1984: the erosion of agricultural soils, acidic precipitation, toxic wastes, the loss of wild and unique places, psychological stress, ethnic and international confrontations, nuclear weapons. . .What are the landmarks for our behavior in 1985? How can we learn from human successes and failures that have marked the land in the past? Humor and imagination, field and forest are part of the art and reality of adaptation to our ever-faster changing environment.

Artist	Specific impacts
Abish	Little specific impact
Aycock	Mercury spill & vapor hazard
Denes	Sharp projections a hazard to people & animals
Feigenbaum	Soil erosion, siltation of stream in ravine, opening secluded ravine to more intensive use
Ferrara	Little specific impact
Fleischner	Little specific impact
The Harrisons	Little specific impact
Holt	Visible from river and main campus; could encourage appreciation of scenery
Mendieta	Introduction of a non-native plant which could spread
Morris	Little specific impact
Oppenheim	Various designs require electricity to operate or potentially toxic wood preservative
Perry	Annual application of toxic turpentine
Pinto	Possible introduction of non-native plants (species not stated), projecting spikes of wheel hazardous
Ross	Little specific impact
Singer	Opening secluded ravine to more intensive use; soil erosion along trail
Sonfist	Tower visible from river and main campus?; introduction of non-native plants ("tree fragments")?
Stackhouse	Little specific impact
Stuart	Toxicity of gunite?
Tacha	Introduction to site of non-native plants? (not specified); soil erosion and siltation of stream
Thea	Little specific impact, possibly soil erosion & dust along road

Table 1. Some potential environmental impacts of the **Land Marks** *pieces. Most, perhaps all, of the pieces would involve some removal of soil, vegetation, and wildlife habitat, and most would involve short-term damage to soil and vegetation from construction equipment. The pieces also represent a significant consumption of materials and energy for construction.*

Fields of Vision

Shelley Rice

Much has been written about the revived interest in landscape art in America since the 1960s. Though landscape as a genre of the visual arts has never really gone out of fashion in this country, it has taken on new life and meaning since people like Robert Smithson, Michael Heizer and Walter De Maria decided to discard their canvases and traditional sculptural materials and use the earth itself as their medium. The works of these men are well known and well documented, but now that almost twenty-five years have passed since Earthworks came into being, it is time to look closely at the site sculptures being produced today, either by the first generation of earth artists or by the younger people who have entered the field in recent years. The **Land Marks** exhibition allows us to do just that: to assess the thought processes of these artists in the 1980s, and to place their ideas within the context of the art of the recent and the more distant past.

Aspects of the past are very relevant for an understanding of current Earthworks, since this art is part of a tradition which has served an important role in American life. During the early years of this country's history, the vast scale of the land, its awesome range, diversity and richness was a challenge for settlers; the wilderness posed problems of survival, not aesthetics. As Joshua C. Taylor put it: "The first appraisals of American nature were made with an eye toward production: how a patch of landscape would favor agriculture, settlement, shipping or prosperity in general. Of course, there were remarks about agreeable vistas and natural curiosities, but the wilderness was there to be won, not admired."[1] That attitude had changed significantly by the early years of the 19th century, as more and more people moved Westward and industrialism became a force in American life, and questions arose as to the relationship between human beings and the land they inhabited. It was at this point that landscape art began to flourish.

Landscape art has, therefore, gained currency at important times of crisis and change in our country's history, times when we have needed some answers to questions about the relationship between humans, nature and technology. That was true in the 19th century, especially in the years between 1825 and 1885; it is true now. In both of these eras, persistent anxieties about our relationship to the land have been pressing issues; in both, artists have attempted to mediate between nature and culture, to realize visions and express ideas which could help us inhabit our environment more effectively. They have attempted to provide the philosophic, moral and spiritual foundations for our tenancy on the land—a land that looks very different, and poses very different problems, for us today than it did in the 19th century. So a comparison between the products of these two "Golden Ages of Landscape" can yield much information, not only about art, but about the continuities and changes of our cultural history.

Both critics and historians have commented on the relationships between Earthworks and their 19th century precedents in landscape painting. In this essay, I would like to focus on another form of 19th-century imagery that has been given short shrift in these art historical discussions, and that I believe is relevant to current concerns: photography. Though landscape photographs were taken of the East Coast (by people like Frederick Langenheim) and the frontier earlier in the medium's history, landscape photography flourished in the American West between 1860 and 1885—a period which Weston Naef has called the "Era of Exploration,"[2] Landscape photography came into its own later than landscape painting, and it borrowed many painterly conventions; many photographers during those years (for instance, A.J. Russell) had at least some training in painting, and others, like Carleton Watkins, Eadweard Muybridge and W.H. Jackson, worked with and were influenced by painters like Bierstadt, Moran and Gifford as they developed personal photographic styles. Because of superficial formal similarities, and because of prejudices against the medium within the art world, photography is usually relegated to a subordinate position in discussions of the history of landscape art. But if one approaches the images from more than a purely formal point of view, it is quite clear that the men who documented the wilderness with the camera were working with an entirely different medium—which served a very different purpose within the culture.

First of all, it must be pointed out that the exalted status enjoyed by painters in 19th-century American society was not shared by photographers. The men whose images are sought after by major museums today were, in their time, perceived simply as workers with a camera—even if some of them, like Watkins and Muybridge, did earn both acclaim and medals here and abroad. Many of the most important landscape photographs of these years were made "for hire," by imagemakers employed by government surveys (Jackson, Timothy O'Sullivan) or by the railroad companies (Russell, Alexander Gardner). Even men who worked independently for the most part, like Watkins and Muybridge, were interested primarily in making a living through sales to speculative clients or to a popular market; the reproducibility of their pictures made wide distribution possible (in the form of prints, books, stereographs and later even postcards), so their images did much to increase the public's knowledge about and awareness of the American wilderness. By spreading ideas directly into the culture-at-large, these photographs had a considerable impact on the actual process of settlement in the West. And it is this aspect of photography's history that will concern us here.

The 19th century landscape photographer's primary function was to document people's progress into the wilderness—and to help make that progress possible. This goal automatically puts them at odds with the earliest landscape painters, like Thomas Cole, whose foremost aims were to communicate the exalted moral sentiments inherent in our virgin land. The 19th century predilection for perceiving God in nature is well known; as Barbara Novak put it: "In the early 19th century in America, nature couldn't do without God, and God apparently couldn't do without nature. By the time Emerson wrote *Nature* in 1836, the terms "god" and "nature" were often the same thing, and could be used interchangeably."[3] This attitude toward nature and the rise of landscape painting, however, coincided with the rapid expansion of civilization and industrialization—and the concurrent destruction of the wilderness which William Cullen Bryant called God's first temple. Inherent in 19th century nature worship was this paradox, and the discomfort it caused can be seen as the motivating force behind the creation of many of the major works of art and literature of the period. Artists were well aware, as *The Literary World* pointed out in 1847, that "The axe of civilization is busy with our old forests, and artisan ingenuity is fast sweeping away the relics of our national infancy . . .Yankee enterprise has little sympathy with the picturesque, and it behooves our artists to rescue from its grasp the little that is left, before it is too late."[4]

The conflict between nature and culture showed itself, not often and then usually discretely, in 19th century landscape painting. Most painters chose to downplay evidence of human incursion into the wilderness: by tucking trains away in the corners of pictures, blending farms bucolically into natural scenes, or depicting burnt tree stumps as evidence of human presence and its latent destructiveness. But the photographers who came on the scene later, lugging their own image-making technology, were a different generation with a different outlook on "Yankee enterprise." Though many of them were concerned about preservation, and all shared the religious awe of the sublime aspects of nature, they were still implicitly on the side of progress, technology and civilization. Many of them, like Russell, Jackson and O'Sullivan had originally come from the East Coast and moved west with the advancing hoards to seek new opportunities; several of them worked with or were influenced by scientists, natural historians and geologists, those secular priests whose discoveries were altering the religious ideas which dominated 19th century perceptions of nature; most of them sought jobs with government agencies exploring wilderness lands for the purpose of settlement and use; and almost all of them, at one time or another, photographed the railroad —the ultimate "Machine in the Garden," to quote the title of Leo Marx's excellent book.[5]

As Weston Naef has written, "The railroad linking Omaha to San Francisco was the primary force behind the burst of outdoor photography that took place in the wake of the Civil War and brought photographers in touch with the land . . ."[6] Far from perceiving the railroad as an intruding element on an idealized landscape, the photographers perceived it as a central factor in their interaction with, and access to, the Western territories. The Union Pacific provided some of these image-makers (like Russell and Gardner) with jobs, and others (like A.A. Hart, C.R. Savage, Jackson, Watkins and Muybridge) with a speculative commercial market for stereographs and prints, since the railroad's construction had sparked tremendous public interest in both the rails and the lands through which they passed. It also provided them with an opportunity to confront directly the relationship between humans, nature and technology. Some of their pictures, like Russell's "Driving of the Golden Spike, Promontory, Utah, 10 May 1869," are documentary photographs emphasizing human triumph over nature; others, like Hart's "Alcove in Palisades, Ten Mile Cañon, 1868," use the railroad to show how tiny human endeavor seems when placed within the grand arena of nature. Still others, many others, focus on the railroad tracks: those regular units of measurement which by 1869 had spanned a continent, and had subjugated the wilds of nature to human intelligence and will.

Nineteenth century "pure" landscape photography, though not explicitly concerned with technology, must be seen within this context: like the railroad tracks, these pictures were a way to exercise this country's passion for measurement and control. The photographers who entered the western regions to record landscape, either as part of survey expeditions or on their own initiative, were delineating territories that had been entered only rarely, supplying information about geographic features and landmarks that could serve as orientation points in unknown lands. Sometimes their pictures, by alerting people to the incomparable beauty of the wilderness, served to literally realize *The Literary World's* exhortation to "rescue the little that is left, before it is too late." During the 1860s, for instance, a set of Watkin's Yosemite photographs which belonged to Senator John Conness influenced Congress to cede Yosemite to the state of California for ecological reasons. And in 1871, an album of Jackson's photographs entitled *Yellowstone's Scenic Wonders,* assembled after the 1871 Hayden Survey, was distributed to influential members of Congress; on the strength of this documentary evidence of our country's scenic wonders, a bill was introduced and passed which set Yellowstone aside as the first national park.[7]

This extraordinary story says much about the impact of photographs in 19th-century America. The members of Congress who voted to make Yellowstone a national park had never physically been there; their only knowledge of this land was photographic. But the truthfulness of photographic evidence was never questioned during those years; and the expanded perception of space made possible by the invention of photography gave these congressmen a control over the wilderness as surely as the railroad did, for on the strength of Jackson's images they exercised a legal power over this environment that has fundamentally altered the quality of life and land in America to this day. In this case the photographs, like the national parks, saved a fundamental aspect of the American landscape before it was too late. But the expansion of human space perception brought on by photography was a double-edged sword. For though in some cases photographs aided in the preservation of virgin lands, in others they encouraged the advent of civilization and the wilderness' concomitant disappearance. The railroads might have provided *physical* access to the western territories—but these images provided *perceptual* and *conceptual* access. By expanding the sense perceptions of American citizens, by giving people a knowledge of and therefore a power over distant and unclaimed lands, these pictures helped to create the conditions conducive to settlement and habitation.

For these photographs served a *naming* function: they isolated, literally brought into focus, certain sites and geographical areas, and gave these landmarks the status of signposts which guided the American public's growing understanding of the West. By making available authentic, objective evidence of what was "out there," these pictures provided (as no idealized painting ever could) an accurate map of these regions which extended human intellectual control over the wilderness long before trees were cut down, roads were built and towns established. Yellowstone, Yosemite, El Capitan, Skull Rock, Perched Rock, the Canon de Chelle, the Mountain of the Holy Cross: all of these sites become familiar to the public, part of the collective image-bank, long before most non-native Americans had ever physically seen or experienced them. But these photographers did more than simply document particular geographical features: they also shouldered the burden of shaping a vision of the philosophic and metaphysical implications of the lands they had chosen to explore. By establishing a set of visual/metaphoric relationships within their picture planes, these image-makers defined, for the public, the meaning of individual landmarks and areas within the overall scheme of nature.

This vision was, of course, influenced greatly by popular conceptions of landscape of their era; it was also influenced by earlier European and American paintings and photographs. But its final manifestation depended greatly on the sensibility and training of the different men involved. Watkins, for instance, who was the pioneer photographer of this Golden Age of landscape, got his visual education in Robert Vance's San Francisco studio, where he had access to hundreds of stereographs, many of them by European masters like Francis Frith, Charles Soulier and the Bisson brothers. His photographs express a vision of nature based on this aesthetic, a vision as classically balanced, self-contained and harmonious as a Claudian landscape. Muybridge, out to compete with Watkins' success, expressed a completely different point of view—a view which emphasized the dynamism, awesome scale and drama of the American landscape. And O'Sullivan, whose eye was most influenced by his experience as a Civil War photographer and his association with geologer Clarence King, probed the landscape to ascertain its underlying structure, while simultaneously presenting the spectator with quantities of minute geological detail and a heightened sense of the layers of time embodied in natural and human history.

Yet for our purposes, these differences are less important than an essential similarity: all of these men "tamed" the land, not literally but with their cameras. By choosing to document certain sites, by setting up a series of relationships within the confines of a picture plane, these photographers made order out of chaos, art out of life: they found and *framed* a vision of the landscape. This framing of the lands can be seen as the visual analogue to what the surveying expeditions were doing; like the surveyors and explorers they accompanied, these photographers isolated, measured and ordered a wilderness. Without altering the environment in the least, they defined the parameters and the meaning of the Western territories for a fascinated public. The impact of this wide distribution of objective "evidence" about the West cannot be overestimated, for these visual images provided a stepping stone to the physical conquest of our land.

And on this level, whatever the difference in form, content and circumstances, these 19th-century landscape photographers can be seen as precursors of the works in the **Land Marks** exhibition. Like the projects in the show, these photographs served as *proposals*—documents of specific sites which laid the groundwork for the future land use of an entire continent. Implicit in their production was a complex vision of nature, culture and technology which, when physically acted upon, gave rise to the reality we know of—for better or worse—as America today. By providing the impetus and information necessary for laws, explorations and settlements, these two-dimensional images helped to shape the physical development of our land, and our nation: an Earthwork-in-progress a continent (and more) wide.

Contemporary earth artists (like the rest of us) are living with the legacy of the 19th-century photographers, and because of that their work must be seen as a dialogue—however indirect—with the work of these image-makers from the past. These photographers shaped a vision of a country that has been acted upon, and has in turn given rise to new dilemmas and challenges which are the motivating forces behind the land art that has flourished in the past few decades. The subjugation of nature, the destruction of the wilderness, the settling of the lands, the willful disregard of ecology: all of these are the birthrights of these 20th-century artists, and their work must be seen as an attempt to come to terms with their forebears' excesses, to correct the imbalances of their vision before it is too late.

The pioneers of 20th-century earth art—like Robert Smithson, Michael Heizer and Walter De Maria—were in many ways close in spirit to the 19th-century pioneers (of art and life). However different their concerns and personal iconographies, all of these artists were involved with massive projects in wide open, preferably uninhabited spaces and often inhospitable and inaccessible terrains. In an almost ritual re-enactment of the westward expansion of civilization, the artists chose their sites and proceeded to alter the landscape, often (in the case of Smithson and Heizer) disrupting the earth in the process with powerful industrial equipment. Their monumental projects were grand gestures in the wilderness which once again transformed nature into culture—and which, most important, opened up a Pandora's box full of questions about the relationship between humans, nature and technology.

The artists represented in the **Land Marks** exhibition have, over the years, addressed these questions, but most of them have done so with a change of circumstance which is very relevant for the art they have produced. Some of these artists (Nancy Holt, Michael Singer and Charles Ross, for instance) have created projects in inaccessible locations, but many of these latter-day earth artists have chosen to make site sculptures which directly confront the issues of human habitation and participation. They have chosen to accept the fact that the conditions of this country have changed: that there is no longer a frontier, that we somehow have to stop and take stock of the truism that humans, nature and technology must learn to cohabit in a finite amount of space. And they have also, many of them, begun to realize that the grand gestures of our forebears have left us with a string of ecological disasters which must be corrected if this planet is to remain viable for life.

These changed circumstances are what make the **Land Marks** exhibition such a fascinating experiment. All twenty of these artists were asked to propose a work for a specific, pre-selected site on the Bard campus: a finite site which is in the midst of a space set aside for human use. Part of the land is cultivated, part uncultivated—but all of it is part of, and has its meaning within, the context of human society and civilization. In creating their projects, all of these people had to grapple with the implications of this interaction between art and life, nature and culture.

This assignment, therefore, confronted them with a challenge that is very much in tune with dominant concerns of the 1980s, and that sets their task almost in diametric opposition to the task faced by the 19th-century landscape photographers. The photographers were faced with wild and almost virgin territory, and it was their job to create meaning where there was none before. By isolating certain landmarks and framing a vision of the wilderness, these image-makers forged the conceptual and perceptual *boundaries* which literally made order out of chaos. Confronted with huge expanses of uninhabited territory, with almost unlimited fields of vision, their task involved a process of *closure:* a closing down of certain possibilities and points of view so that others could come to fruition.

The artists in this exhibition, on the other hand, have no need for closure; the process of settling and civilizing this country has effectively limited their possibilities. They are faced instead with a need for *expansion*—in art as well as life. The urge for expansion gave rise to the Earthworks of the 1960s; artists rejected traditional media and the context of galleries and museums as being too limited, and felt instead that they could make more relevant statements about the relations between nature and culture in a non-art environment, for a non-art audience. All subsequent earth artists have been involved in this breaking down of boundaries between art and life—and, by extension, in the breaking down of boundaries which limit our definitions of the land. Given a site which has already been assigned a use and meaning within the context of the Bard campus (and thus contemporary society), all of the artists in the exhibition have proposed using that site, in one way or another, to expand our perceptual understanding of the role of the land, and our relationship to it.

In a way, this expanded perception is the new, 20th-century frontier. Whereas the 19th-century photographers created works which set the stage for the conquest of a continent, these 20th-century artists are attempting to alter our conception of the land, and however three-dimensional and physical their work, their pioneering efforts must be in the realm of the mind. We have no more room to move in; now we must rethink our relationship with what we have, and break down the 19th-century ways of perceiving the earth which have led to great accomplishments but which are also, at this stage, leading us headlong toward ecological and social disaster. So while the 19th-century image-makers were out to dominate and order nature, to celebrate human achievement and make our triumph over the wilderness possible, these 20th-century artists are faced with the urgent necessity of trying to restore a balance, a series of mutually agreeable relationships, between human beings and the world in which they live. And they are doing so by conceptually recontextualizing a particular site within the larger contexts of human society, history, ecology, even the stars—expanding its meaning so that we the viewers can understand that it is part of a complex series of relationships which together create the conditions for human existence.

There is a strong element of fantasy involved in the **Land Marks** exhibition. Though these projects may be realized at some point in the future, the exhibition called only for proposals—drawings, models, statements, etc.—for site sculptures, and without the restrictions of budget, time considerations, labor and material costs the artists were free to let their imaginations run free. They were restricted only by the limitations of the site chosen by Linda Weintraub, the curator of the show, who described the land as follows: "It is a 5.7 acre field with a gentle slope. It is surrounded on three sides by trees and on one side by a road which is opposite the art gallery. The work can be designed to be set in the woods or in the open area—on a mowed field or one that is allowed to grow naturally."[8]

So the artists were given a choice of terrain: they could design a project for a mowed field, a natural one or the woods; for flat ground or sloped. Interestingly enough, the majority of the artists chose to work in the field, and to create sculptures of one kind or another within this space. Also noteworthy is the fact that few artists chose to significantly disrupt or alter the landscape *á la* Smithson; most of the projects sit on top of the earth, and any damage caused by the construction of the site work would be smoothed over or repaired. Beyond these few observations, however, one cannot generalize about unifying themes, formal devices, materials or methods of construction. The diversity of these proposals is truly remarkable.

This diversity extends to the role that people—the implied viewers—play in the works. In 19th-century Western landscape photography, as in 19th-century landscape painting, figures—when they appeared at all—were often depicted as minute in comparison to the vast scale of nature. Since all of the **Land Marks** artists are working with a site geared to human scale within a defined social environment, people loom large in their proposals by implication. Many of these site works are, in fact, experiential: they are not simply designed to be looked at, but to be physically used, entered, climbed upon, etc. by viewers engaged in a "real" time and space experience.

Both Richard Fleischner and Jackie Ferrara, for instance, have proposed structures which, in Fleischner's words, serve as "a destination and place within the field."[9] But after assessing the site, these two artists have chosen very different forms and very different ways of relating people to their environment. Fleischner's "Stone Block Construction," which would be composed of a series of large, pink grey granite blocks, has a simple structure which makes it almost primitive in feeling; its portals and almost enclosed spaces, however minimal, remind one of the archaeological ruins of ancient homes. Predominantly horizontal, the piece rambles over the landscape and invites the viewer to do the same: to walk through its portals, amble in its spaces and relax on stone surfaces geared very much to human scale.

Jackie Ferrara's "2-D 78 Bard Platform," like Fleischner's work, would be composed primarily of natural materials—cedar boards—that relate the work to its environment. But Ferrara's piece is an L-shaped monolithic form which functions vertically rather than horizontally. There are a number of different levels built into this platform: a concrete deck near the ground, a cedar "floor" at the top, and stairs moving up the sides of the piece which link the two. As the spectator ascends, s/he experiences different views not only of the piece but also of the surrounding countryside. Besides providing a series of perceptual experiences, the floors and steps can also serve as stages for performances—a gesture by the artist that takes account of the nearby Bard Theater.

Cecile Abish also took account of the Theater; her "Epicurean Arrangements," named after a passage from Friedrich Nietzsche's *The Gay Science,* would have a raised cedar deck as one of its component parts. But Abish's work is not about objects: it is about relationships between objects and spaces. Her landscaping proposal creates a series of interlocking and interrelated forms and spaces which echo each other on a formal level and thus, in the artist's words, "initiate an archetype" which charges the entire area with meaning. The raised deck is balanced by the sunken lawn opposite it; the diamond shapes of the brick walls with portals resonate in the landscaped designs of gravel paths lined with trees. So the site is transformed into a ritual space in which nature and culture, form and space, two-dimensions and three-dimensions become part of the same continuum.

Michael Singer's wooden "house" structure is also a ritual space, which would provide shelter and solitude in the wooded ravine. Composed of wood and nestling into its environment, the structure has a Japanese flavor—a flavor that is accentuated since it too, like Abish's work, is about the unification of opposites so important in Oriental thought. The structure is closed, but its doors and windows are open onto the environment; inside, the viewer can stand on an upper or lower pathway and contemplate stones which have been raised above or sunken into the earthen floor; the geometric forms of the structure play off of the natural curves of the stones. Open and closed, convex and concave, natural and artificial: all co-exist in balance in this shelter, which invites the viewer to contemplate the harmonious interrelationships of humans and the nature of which they are a part.

Like Singer, Carolee Thea has set her work in the woods. But whereas Singer envisions a single structure, Thea proposes a series of six, life-size bronze sculptures of the mythic Daphne, which would show her fleeing into the forest to allude Apollo and finally metamorphosizing into a tree. This is a narrative work, but the sequential sculptures that chronicle the tale would be spread out over a large area; the viewer would have to walk from sculpture to sculpture, following Daphne's route and thus reliving her flight from civilization and subsequent transformation from mortal to wood nymph. Through this experience, contemporary spectators would be linked up with the mythic past, and cross the boundaries separating culture from nature.

By spreading her sculptures throughout the site, Thea charges the entire ambient landscape with psychological overtones. Harriet Feigenbaum and Athena Tacha have also chosen to use a large area for their works, but instead of putting sculpture on it they have chosen to significantly alter the land by terracing it. By constructing spiral terraces, reminiscent of South American forms, which will catch water on the open field, Feigenbaum wants to create a series of waterfalls and rapids that will pay homage to the proximity of the Hudson and make possible the formation of a shallow lake in the adjacent ravine. Since the lake is designed to be used as a skating rink in winter, the whole area will be transformed, in the artist's words, into "a dramatically landscaped and thoroughly useable park" which will reconcile human pleasures and ecological concerns.

Athena Tacha's terracing, on the other hand, would form the low grassy hill into the general shape of the oak leaves which the artist found on the site. Interspersed on this natural grassy environment would be a number of stepped concrete structures: human-made elements of human scale imposed on the land, and yet echoing the flow and rhythm of its terraced contours. But as viewers climb these step sequences, they will confront photographs and inscriptions embedded in their surfaces which will illustrate both the constructive and the destructive sides of human technological achievements. So the piece is not only a celebration of the harmonious balance of the natural and the human-made, but also a warning that this balance has been, and must not continue to be, disturbed.

Tacha's desire to place this plot of land on the Bard campus within the context of western technological achievement is shared by Robert Morris. But whereas Tacha would create an experiential work, Morris proposes a metaphoric sculpture—quite literally a monument (tongue in cheek, one hopes) to all the clichés about western culture. Consisting of three cylindrical forms with parabolic nose cones, the piece chronicles three stages of human progress (defined as the species' separation from nature and natural materials): the first stone form is embedded in the earth, the second bronze one rises at a 60° angle and the third, made of steel, stands upright. Pointed like a missile, or an erect penis, toward the heavens, the third form is a fitting symbol of the phallocentricity of our contemporary technological civilization.

Agnes Denes's interest in western culture, on the other hand, is purely mathematical. Her tall, thin, umbrella-like pyramidal sculpture in red, black and silver, entitled "Pascal's Triangle: Systems of Logic/Logic of Systems," would be a steel cable suspension structure which would visualize the number expansion of Pascal's triangle. By taking the universal concepts of mathematics and translating them into physical form, the artist is attempting to reveal the continuity of the patterns which govern both mind and matter.

Like Agnes Denes, Dennis Oppenheim is interested in the relationship between mind and matter, and the four sculptures he designed for the exhibition visualize his conception of intangible physical or mental states. "Rolling Explosion," for instance, which would be made of steel and aluminum, is (in the artist's words) "a mobile abacus that constantly radiates then contracts as it journeys along a track"; it represents, not literal fact, but Oppenheim's visualization of a molecular explosion. "Roots in Cubism. Hearts in the Stars. (Forest for Cezanne)," on the other hand, would use both natural and human-made materials—wood, stone, steel and cement—to visualize the geometric structures within trees which Cezanne perceived en route to his discovery of Cubism. Matter and mind, objects and the visual perception of them, merge here in a sculptural illusion, unified by metal arcs which, in the artist's words, "indicate comet trails from celestial origins."

"Celestial origins" are right up Alice Aycock's alley. Aycock's "A Representation of the Second World" would consist of three identical models of a fantasy world, contained within 24′ and 28′ concentric glass bowls partially embedded in the ground and complete with a concrete island Earth, Terrestrial Oceans filled with mercury (poor fish) and a watery Underworld. Three concentric rings rotate around each of these parallel universes, whose earth chambers are conneced by an underground passage which can be crawled through but whose dimensions (2′ high and wide) would make the journey both difficult and terrifying.

Like Aycock, Jody Pinto has proposed building three large and potentially experiential structures. But whereas Aycock is visualizing a complex and fantastic world picture, Pinto is using iconography from western history and mythology to make humorous comments on the relationship between nature and culture. Her "Five-Spoke Seeded Catherine Wheel" refers to the wheel which tortured this Christian martyr—but the piece would transform a device of religious discipline into a cracked cement and rot treated timber ruin which, when seeded, would look like a big hairy spider. Her "Tower for the Study of Languages," on the other hand, is a large phallic symbol with forked tongues protruding from it. This contemporary Tower of Babel might be a monument to speech ("the capacity that defines us as sovereign over nature," in the artist's words), but its pinnacles are only humanly attainable with a hoist and chair.

Pinto's reference to the study of languages places this work not only within the context of cultural history but also within the immediate social context of education at Bard College—a theme also pursued by Michelle Stuart. Stuart proposes building a huge—24 × 30′—"The Bard's Song Book" on the open field. Like Pinto, Stuart is playing with both language and cultural history here; her statement reads: "One hopes that students in whatever field they choose, will be the poets of their time and maybe for all time. One praises the book . . . be it history or legend . . . but one praises more the song of the Bard." This massive volume would have a steel frame which would be sprayed with gunite and colored and textured with earth chosen by the artist. So this book of knowledge would literally grow out of the land on which it rests, and incorporate the artist's gestures and responses to the natural soil in the environment.

Beatrice Perry is also responding to the environment, but her large stainless steel and corten steel sculpture (composed of nine freestanding parts) uses abstract forms designed to evoke field and mountain, in sizes, shapes and relationships determined by the contour of the terrain and the surrounding trees and buildings. Made of industrial materials, this sculpture would nevertheless reflect the ambient landscape, changing color with the light and the seasons.

Sensitivity to the environment leads us to ecological concerns. Though most of the artists in this show are concerned with ecological issues and the harmonizing of nature and culture, Alan Sonfist and the Harrisons have been particularly active in this area over the years. Sonfist's three projects are involved with recycling nature, and with fostering awareness of the balances and diversity of indigenous natural environments. His "Endless Column" is a tower built of fallen tree fragments, cast in bronze, that represent native trees all over the USA and include samples from the Bard area. This cross-section of our national environment would be complemented by "Circle of Life," an in-depth examination of the cycle of the Bard area forest. Representative indigenous trees would form a circle on the field, in the center of which would be a series of columns of fallen limbs (bronze cast) from the Bard forest.

By analyzing native vegetation, "Circle of Life" promotes understanding of one of the ecological systems which together make up a natural environment. Helen and Newton Harrison are particularly concerned with the ways that human civilization and technology are destroying the delicate balance of ecological systems, and their "Still Pure Water" project would make it clear that human beings can cooperate with nature to achieve their goals. A barn-like structure that stores warmth, "Still Pure Water" would utilize the water from the environment, which would condense on its glass roof and then move through the system. The end result: pure water, available for drinking through a spigot in the gallery.

Whereas Sonfist deals with vegetation cycles and the Harrisons with water cycles, Robert Stackhouse is concerned with the cycles of history, the cultural forms that have lived and died, in the Bard area. His "Hudson Prospect/River Bones" would be a large, aluminum, ship-like shape, patinaed white, with horizontal planks supporting vertical posts. This "ship," which the artist would situate in a low area that could fill with water when it rains, would contain within its structure references to the now defunct whaling history of the Hudson: its skeletal form echoes the bare bones of both the ships and the whales that once thrived in the region, and the standing posts (cast from local pilings, and including their barnacles) would be reminiscent of grave markers. So the piece would be, in the artist's words, "a ruin . . . a graveyard of Hudson River history."

Ana Mendieta is also concerned with history—or, more properly speaking, herstory. Her "La Maja de Yerba" aspires to go beyond recent human history and connect us with, in her words, "the void, the orphanhood, the unbaptized earth of the beginning." By drawing a large (9 × 5′) female form directly upon the land, by creating this form out of spirals (shapes which are simultaneously open and closed in upon themselves) and by planting seedlings upon this drawing, Mendieta is attempting to tap into, and affirm, the ancient ties that bind nature and the mythic female body.

Whereas Mendieta is concerned with the primordial beginnings of the earth, both Nancy Holt and Charles Ross seek to find the connections between earth and sky. Both of their pieces are about observation—about the ways in which human visual perception forges links between individuals and the larger universe of which they are a part. Holt's "O Silo" is an experiential work consisting of eight silo-like structures of concrete and steel with central circular openings inspired by similar structures in the countryside around Bard. As the spectator approaches various "lookout points" (the viewing platform 90′ above the ground, a subterranean passage, the circular openings in the silos of different heights) from various points of view, aspects of the environment (the landscape, the river, the ground, the sky) come into focus. But these silos are themselves aligned with the sunsets and sunrises on the summer and winter solstices and the equinoxes. As a result, the viewer's momentary perceptions, nature, the sky and the history and culture of the area are brought into alignment through the perceptual experience of the piece.

Charles Ross, like Holt, is interested in alignments of heaven and earth—but his main concern is to "bring the motion of the stars to personal measure, so we can feel the unity of the movement of the universe in relation to ourselves."[10] The very shape of his piece, which would be constructed primarily of reinforced aggregate concrete, was determined in relation to the stars, and it provides the viewer with several different perceptual experiences. As the spectator looks upward from the observing stone, s/he is oriented toward the celestial north. Yet this fixed orientation is counterpointed from another perspective, for as the viewer stands within the spectrum chamber, the movement of light through a prism and across the chamber literally lets him/her see and feel the turning of the earth.

In both Nancy Holt's and Charles Ross's works, the viewer/observer becomes the center of the world: the nexus point where nature, culture, the land and the sky come into alignment to find their meaning within the human psyche. Both artists behold a universe enormous in scale and even mystical in implication; but both also perceive the human viewer of that universe as an integral part of its creative force. And this, finally, separates them—and the rest of the artists in the exhibition—from their 19th-century predecessors.

The tiny figures who contemplate the landscape or simply stand within it as barometers of scale in 19th-century landscape photographers are dwarfed by its size and magnificence. Conversely, when men are depicted as having conquered nature, as they are in certain documentary railroad photographs, they are shown large and triumphant. The unequal power balance between nature and humans perceived by 19th-century Americans gave rise to an either-or situation, a kill-or-be-killed mentality which in all ways separated us off from nature. But recent awareness of ecological issues, of the ties which bind us to the earth and other life forms, of the give and take which must necessarily govern all of our actions or lead to disaster, has humbled us on the other hand—and aggrandized us on the other. For if we are, indeed, part of nature, we share its awesome force; thought we might not be, in Renaissance parlance, "the measure of all things," we do share front row seats at the center of our world. And this dual awareness, of both our humility and our power, infuses almost all of the works in the **Land Marks** exhibition.

The artists represented here are not, like their 19th-century photographic forebears, popular image-makers; their work will not go into the mainstream of mass culture and significantly influence, in a direct way, the fate of our continental lands. But they are, like Watkins, Jackson and Muybridge, shaping the way we see things and thus, hopefully, laying the foundations for a future in which the dichotomy between human beings and their environment is resolved in favor of balance, cooperation and harmony. And in this sense their works are proposals, not only for site sculptures, but also for a new world in which both nature and culture can survive.

---

[1]Joshua C. Taylor, "A Land for Landscapes," in Alan Sonfist, editor, *Art in the Land: A Critical Anthology of Environmental Art* (New York: E.P. Dutton, Inc., 1983) pp. 1-2.

[2]Weston Naef, in collaboration with James N. Wood, *Era of Exploration: The Rise of Landscape Photography in the American West, 1860-1886,* ex. cat. (New York: Albright-Knox Art Gallery and The Metropolitan Museum of Art, 1975).

[3]Barbara Novak, *Nature and Culture: American Landscape and Painting, 1825-1875* (New York: Oxford University Press, 1980), p. 3.

[4]Quoted in Perry Miller, "Nature and the National Ego," in *Errand into the Wilderness* (New York: Harper & Row, 1964), pp. 205-6.

[5]Leo Marx, *The Machine in the Garden: Technology and the Pastoral Ideal in America* (New York: Oxford University Press, 1964).

[6]Weston Naef, op.cit., p. 42.

[7]For more information on this, see Weston Naef, op.cit., p. 73 and Robert Taft, *Photography and the American Scene* (New York: Dover Publications, Inc., 1964), pp. 299-302.

[8]Linda Weintraub, from an unpublished letter sent to the **Land Marks** artists.

[9]Richard Fleischner, from his "Statement" for the **Land Marks** exhibition catalogue. From this point on, unless otherwise noted, all artists' quotes are from their catalogue statements.

[10]Charles Ross, from an unpublished book describing "Star Axis," a work-in-progress by this artist being constructed in New Mexico.

Parallel Evolution in Site Art and Ecology

Daniel Simberloff

What Are Site Art and Ecology, and Where Did They Come From?

Land Marks invites consideration of what "site art" is, and why we view it as an exciting, innovative aspect of twentieth century art. It is not, of course, just that these works are outdoors. The large Easter Island *ahu* statues are outdoors, yet we would not likely view them as lineal ancestors of current site sculpture. Hellenic buildings and statues were often in superb natural settings. The Temple of Poseidon and associated kouroi at Sounion, combined with the magnificent promontory on which they were located, presented the most striking appearance from both land and sea. Nonetheless, we would not seek antecedents to modern site sculpture and earthworks at Sounion. The scale and setting of Mount Rushmore are as expansive as those of our most heralded modern site works, yet Craig Adcock[1] scoffs at Borglum and sees him as unrelated to current earth artists. He feels it was not Borglum's message that was faulty, but that he said it in an *old* way. The best recent earth art, by contrast, has an old message, but the message is transmitted in a new, sophisticated way.

Just what the old message and new communicatory mode are is not stated, nor are we told in what sense recent workers are more sophisticated. I would argue that the key is the "site" in "site art." The works at Easter Island, Sounion, and Mount Rushmore would not qualify as "site art" because they are not intimately tied to their respective sites. The Temple of Poseidon would have to be near the sea, and Borglum's conception required rock faces as massive as those of the Black Hills, but these are wide constraints, and each of the three works could as well have been located in Fort Lee. On the other hand, the vegetated, predominantly mangrove islets of Christo's "Surrounded Islands" are very uncommon; only in parts of south Florida and the West Indies are there similar archipelagoes. Nancy Holt's "Sun Tunnels" could have been placed only in a vast desert, and only certain vast deserts at that. The shifting dunes of most African deserts, for example, would have prevented the "locators"[2] of "Sun Tunnels" from locating anything, and openings of the tunnels are oriented towards specific mountains. Robert Smithson's "Spiral Jetty" was so intimately tied to the Great Salt Lake that it could have been constructed nowhere else. Its rocks and salt crystals were those of its site, its receding spiral mirrored the curved, receding shoreline, the salt that crystallized on the jetty often does so in spirals, and a local legend connects the lake to the ocean by a spiraling whirlpool.[3]

John Beardsley[4] argues that what is new is a shift, begun in the mid-1960s, from using the landscape as background to engaging it as an integral part of the art. He observes that this shift coincided with enhanced popular interest in the natural environment and how humans have affected it. I believe that he is correct, but that the popular environmental movement, galvanized in 1962 by Rachel Carsons's description of the recondite ramifications of pesticide use *(Silent Spring),* was itself a consequence of an increasingly mature academic science of ecology that some site artists tapped directly.

Ecology is a young science[5]; the sorts of scientific endeavors that we now classify as "ecology" began in Europe in the late 19th century, while the first American textbook was published in 1900. Initial focus on both continents was on the holism of plant communities—the organization of populations of different species into units with an organic integrity so highly developed that they constitute veritable superorganisms. This conception of nature accorded well with the Platonic notion of the universe (including biotic nature) as an ordered, organized whole, and with a tradition stretching back at least to the pre-Socratic Greeks that saw a manifest balance of nature.[6] Early descriptions of superorganismic plant communities struck a responsive chord. Smuts acknowledged that his philosophy of holism was inspired by the writings of the American ecologist Frederic Clements on plant community organization, while in Europe the Russian ecologist Sukachev propounded ideas very similar to those of Clements with equal impact.

The subsequent development of ecology included three key foci. First was the natural succession of plant communities that proceeds on a barren or cleared site. Second was the site-specific aspects of the biotic community at a given location, and of the succession that leads to that community. Third was the random components of succession and community composition. Although progress in all three areas has only imperfectly filtered into the popular environmental movement, site art has incorporated these foci.

Clements and Sukachev analogized ecological succession to the different stages in an individual life cycle; until 1947 this process was the dominant focus of ecology. A plowed field left fallow in the northeastern United States is colonized first by characteristic grass species and other herbs, then by other herbs and shrubs, then by other shrubs and trees, and ultimately by a persistent community, the "climax," comprising certain characteristic tree species. When disturbance intercedes in this succession, by either anthropogenous activities such as agriculture or natural occurrences such as fires, a "disclimax" may be maintained, but the disclimax is not stable. When the disturbance (plowing, burning, etc.) is removed, succession will proceed to the climax, and even if the disturbance is continued, a site may gradually change, as by diminution of soil nutrients or accumulation of toxic phytochemicals, so that the disclimax community cannot be maintained without additional treatment.

Site sculptors and earth artists have studied succession. For example, a diagrammatic treatment is "Time Landscape," in which Alan Sonfist attempted by deliberate planting to recreate three stages of the succession to forest that would occur if New York City were miraculously cleared of human constructions and left a giant field of barren earth. In order to produce "Time Landscape," Sonfist had to learn enough plant ecology to predict what plants would occur at what periods.

Clements, Sukachev, and their followers not only viewed communities as holistic superorganisms, but conceived of succession as a deterministic, community-level process.[7] An entire community replaced another entire community, then persisted *in toto* until it, in turn, was replaced, as a unit, by another community. Furthermore, the whole suite of communities and ultimate climax were the same over an entire region. There was little scope for local site characteristics, historical factors, or chance events to modify the process or its conclusion. In the entire southeastern United States coastal plain an identical longleaf pine-wiregrass community will be achieved except in low, moist sites. Similarly, a monotonous spruce forest will cover much of the northeastern United States and southeastern Canada. Succession will ultimately proceed to the same climax whether it is primary succession (beginning in an abiotic state, as on a lava flow) or secondary succession (beginning from an existing biotic community, as when an old grassy field is left fallow). Clements viewed secondary succession as the superorganismic analog of wound repair, and thus as further evidence for holistic community integrity. Variation among apparent climax plant communities in the same region was viewed as "noise" that obscured an ideal pattern, an aberration to be ignored or at best seen through, rather than as a phenomenon worthy of study in its own right. The first generation of academic ecologists discounted site-specificity, as I have argued above that the antecedents to current earth art were not site-specific.

Increasing accumulation of population- rather than community-level data rendered the Clementsian view progressively less tenable,[8] until, in 1947, a series of plant ecology papers initiated a re-examination of the nature of the community generally and succession and its climax in particular.[9] Although this re-examination is still underway, it was clear even a decade ago that some tenets must be revised, all of which render communities and succession more site-specific and also introduce chance into the successional process. First, communities are not nearly so holistic as was originally believed. Communities are primarily just collections of species with similar physical requirements. A few plant species may affect or even partly constitute the physical environment, and most of the other species are just along for the ride. Second, succession is a population process, not a community one. Species come and species go, but not as integrated groups. One can rarely see community A quickly replaced by community B. Instead, at varying rates, populations of species in community A decrease, while populations of species in community B increase; the designations "community A" and "community B" are arbitrary. Third, there is an inherent site-to-site variation among successions, even in the same region. Minor climatic and edaphic differences are reflected in different species compositions of communities and differences in rates and endpoints of succession. The biotic history of a site matters, so that secondary succession need not lead to the same climax as primary succession would have. Seeds in the soil, for example, or soil nutrient levels determined by previous agricultural practices, can modify the climax community that will ultimately occupy a site.

Earth artists in the last fifteen years have assimilated the population-level nature and site-specificity of succession. For example, the "ecological narratives" of Helen and Newton Harrison constitute artistic renditions of the successional process and emphasize population phenomena. "Barrier Islands" describes the birth, vegetational succession, and death of barrier islands as a natural process. "Thinking about the Mangrove and the Pine" treats the threat to the mangrove climax of south Florida by the introduced Australian pine *(Casuarina)* and human habitation. The harmful effects of the exotic tree are certainly not apparent to casual observers, many of whom view *Casuarina* as a soft, attractive windbreak and mangrove swamps as muddy, mosquito-ridden hellholes. Yet, as the Harrisons depict, the mangrove is a superbly adapted natural climax community on tropical muddy shores, while *Casuarina,* poorly adapted to the winds and waves of the Florida coast, is easily uprooted, with supratidal land subsequently washing into the sea. That the destruction of mangrove swamps is a population- rather than community-level process is apparent from the fact that a single exotic tree species replaces a few mangrove plant species that provide the physical substrate for the rest of the community.

Many artists have expressed their concern for the specific nature of each site. Nancy Holt, for example, aims to perceive the "essence" of each site,[10] and feels that her art includes its site as an essential part of her work.[11] Her concern is ecological, as when it focusses attention on hydrological cycles ("Catch Basin"), but she also studies anthropological and astronomical aspects of each site. Charles Ross's "Star Axis—Where the Earth Meets the Sky" in the New Mexican desert rests on a precise understanding of the unique projection of stars at each spot on the surface of the earth. Michelle Stuart's rock and soil rubbings are artistic renderings of the edaphic character of each site, while her increasing integration of photographs into her work (*e.g.,* the "Islas Encantadas" series) relates biotic to geologic nature. I will discuss site specifity at greater length as I deal with the **Land Marks** project.

Plant ecologists can now predict with some assurance tree species in the climax community of any particular site, as well as many component species of earlier successional stages, and can also estimate how long succession will take. They can also predict to some extent the difficulties of maintaining a disclimax and how quickly these difficulties will arise. But there is an inherent stochasticity to succession, so that some predictions can only be statistical, as when a gambler estimates a 1/6 chance that a pair of dice will yield a 7. A secondary succession initiated by a fire in winter may lead to a different climax than one initiated by a summer fire, because different seeds may be available from the surrounding vegetation. A chance storm carrying seeds from an unusual site can lead to a different local succession.

Increasing recognition by ecologists and other scientists of the essential randomness of certain natural phenomena[12] has led to a series of probabilistic or stochastic laws that contrast sharply with the precise determinism of the eighteenth and nineteenth centuries. Stochastic laws *are* laws; at some level there *is* a pattern to nature, but it is a different sort of pattern than that envisioned by, *e.g.,* the Newtonian physics that underlies prediction of celestial trajectories. If we grid a field into quadrats and count raindrops falling in each quadrat, we cannot predict in advance which quadrat will receive the largest number of drops, or even what the largest number is. We can, however, confidently state that a Poisson distribution of drops in quadrats will obtain for the entire ensemble of quadrats, that the variance among quadrats will bear a certain relation to the mean number of drops per quadrat, and that the greatest number of drops in any one quadrat will fall within a certain narrow range of values. Similarly, ecologists have gradually evolved a stochastic view of their discipline, epitomized by laws on competition between two species that give probabilities of different outcomes,[13] and recognize that replicate experiments need not give random aspects, so that its path can only be predicted probabilistically.

Randomness has infiltrated the arts at the same time as it has transformed the sciences, as a general appreciation of the role of chance has spread through all perceptive modalities. Aleatory music is a good example; notes are drawn randomly from a specific statistical distribution. Similarly, Thomas Pynchon's novels develop metaphors for statistical distributions such as the Poisson and explore the way these distributions govern human activity.[14] The increasing role of chance in the visual arts is so well known that it would be superfluous for me to give details. One has only to think of Jackson Pollock's devices—throwing paint, attaching a brush to an animal's tail, etc.—to recognize that randomness received far more attention in the last few decades than it had previously.

Earth art has incorporated the same aspect of stochasticity—randomness within bounds. Smithson's interest in natural entropic processes on a geological time scale presaged this movement. Entropy is not complete chaos, since the increasing disorder conforms to certain statistical distributions. As entropy increases, the location of specific particles and the status of specific regions of a system become less predictable, but one can specify the probabilities of certain arrangements, and one can predict statistical patterns that will be approached.[15] Alice Aycock's works of the mid 1970s included structures fractured into apparently randomly arranged fragments, while her later machines with moving parts, and similar but more explosive constructions by Dennis Oppenheim, are explicit evocations of the tension between order and randomness. Alan Sonfist's tower of leaves is another exquisite example of stochasticity in earth art. From 1965 to 1977, falling leaves were enclosed by a ring of high poles. The exact position of each leaf, and thus the appearance of at least the top of the growing pile, is random, determined by wind and rain at the precise instant of abscission. Thus the stochastic aspect of succession is revealed. However, the general appearance is determined by the trees in the vicinity, and the relative times of abscission for the different species are themselves fixed stochastic traits, so that strata of the tower are forced to have a certain pattern. The overall *facies* of the pile is constrained within a narrow range.

Since prediction of future occurrences according to natural laws, rather than simple description, is the hallmark of scientific activity, one can now say that ecology is a science. Certainly 17th and 18th century botanists could not have predicted the successional process, at least in sites they did not know well, with nearly the accuracy of today's ecologists. Furthermore, we now understand much of the physico-chemical basis for all successions[16]—why they occur—though such matters are beyond the scope of this essay. Of course, many primitive peoples were shifting agriculturists and had some feel for succession. The Wappinger Indians who occupied the vicinity of the **Land Marks** site from ca. 3000 years ago cleared large fields for planting and also used fire to maintain their agricultural disclimax.[17] They recognized that such disclimaxes eventually deteriorate and so moved their villages occasionally. The legacy of this shifting and burning combines with the edaphic diversity[18] and topographic relief to produce the vegetational heterogeneity of the Bard College region—forests of one sort or another interspersed with wetland communities, active and abandoned agricultural fields, and rock outcrops. Some "primitive" tribes of Mexico and Amazonia show even more sophistication, shifting their agricultural sites before productivity falls, interplanting certain crops that facilitate one another's growth, and carrying seeds from site to site so that seed sources are readily available. However, the Indians' knowledge was limited to one region, and their predictions were purely inductive, whereas ecologists today can deduce predictions about many sites from much more fundamental physico-chemical principles, such as the laws of thermodynamics. Again, subsuming many different phenomena under the same general laws and seeking not correlations but "causes" in these laws is the essence of true science.

Perhaps the most ambitious linkage of earth art to the increasingly sophisticated science of ecology is the reconstruction of damaged biotic communities. The Harrisons have been called "reclamation artists,"[19] and have endeavored to integrate their art into projects that reclaim disturbed sites, such as abandoned chemical dumps. Similarly, Harriet Feigenbaum has been concerned in her Dickson City, Pennsylvania, project with reclamation of strip mine spoils. The Surface Mining Control and Reclamation Act of 1977 mandated that abandoned strip mines be restored to a state capable of supporting whatever activities the site was originally used for. This act presented an immense challenge to ecologists, who had to begin to understand what the original biotic community had been and how to reconstruct and maintain it. The enormity of this endeavor cannot easily be grasped except by ecologists. Perhaps the flavor of the enterprise can be conveyed by the fact that the academic literature is rife with examples of subtle linkages between certain species or between species and their physical environments that can only be deduced after years of field research. An entire subdiscipline of ecology has arisen dedicated to restoration of disturbed sites,[20] and some problems may be virtually insoluble. For example, mine tailings of many minerals may so contaminate the soil that many original plant species cannot recolonize even when the mine is abandoned, and the tailings act by natural selection to produce different genotypes of those species that can survive. For an artist to plan, as Feigenbaum did, pine forests and vineyards on abandoned mines requires ecological as well as aesthetic sophistication. One must understand the nature of an ecological community, the process of succession, and ecological site-specificity.

One sees, then, that at several scales, site artists have mirrored ecologists' interests, especially in their increasing recognition of highly localized traits that characterize any site. Artists have been especially concerned with ecological traits, but have treated larger, astronomic features of sites that do not have such direct ecological impacts as do, for example, soil or moisture regimes. Of course, the same celestial geometry that determines the appearance of astronomic bodies from an earthly site also determines the latitude of that site. Latitude in turn affects the ecological community both obviously *(e.g.,* through its effect on temperature) and subtly *(e.g.,* through its effect on daylength at different times of the year, which evolution has turned into a major cue for animal and plant activity cycles). However, I would argue that site artists who have emphasized astronomy, such as Holt and Ross, have yet to treat the linkage between astronomy and ecology, and have exploited astronomic features of sites primarily for aesthetic purposes. Finally, site artists have interested themselves in anthropogenous impacts on ecology, and this interest again has necessitated sensitivity to specific features of each site.

The ***Land Marks*** *Site*

The **Land Marks** site is very unusual to an ecologist, topographically, vegetationally, and even historically. It is a natural triangular stage, bounded on one leg by a steep ravine, on the other (northern) leg by two steep ravines divided by a narrow high wedge, and on its base by a more gentle elevational decline (on which is situated the Blum Gallery). That the field is almost cleared of trees and even shrubs while the sides are all thickly wooded accentuates the stage-like appearance. Finally, the enormous planted white pines *(Pinus strobus)*, particularly the row along the base of the triangle, contrast with the much smaller trees on ravines and behind the base to invest the site with an almost religious magnificence. Were all peripheral constructions removed, I could imagine this site as an altar for giants.

The vegetation bespeaks human intervention. The grassy field, of course, requires frequent mowing, or else it will succeed to shrubs, then forest. Those few trees that remain, particularly the long hedgerow paralleling the base of the triangle (and almost dividing it into a parallelogram and a smaller triangle) and the row of one silver maple *(Acer saccharinum)* and four white ash *(Fraxinus americana)* trees, remain by the apparent whim of gardeners. The enormous white pines are native, though planted; much of the vegetation, however, is exotic. The hedgerow includes *Rosa multiflora* (a Japanese rose used to create thickets), *Lonicera japonica* (Japanese honeysuckle), Asian *Ulmus* (elms) and their hybrids with native elms, and *Pyrus malus* (apple) a native of the western Himalayas, while the bordering ravines and roadsides add *Rhamnus cathartica* (European buckthorn) and *Picea abies* (Norway spruce). Native species outnumber these introduced ones by about four to one, but the foreign influence is still considerably more apparent than in most American forests. I could not identify most of the grasses within the triangle because my site visit did not coincide with their flowering, but I have little doubt that exotic elements would be present. The introductions arrived as ornamentals planted on the large Hudson River estates in the nineteenth century.[21] In addition to this regional influence, humans probably left historical traces specific to the **Land Marks** site. I have already mentioned the Wappinger Indians' activities. Cattle grazed the site in the nineteenth century, perhaps as recently as forty years ago. A garden near the apex of the triangle was managed by students about a decade ago, while another site near the apex may at one time have been a tree nursery for the college. All these activities affected soil and seed banks in ways that would help to mold present vegetation.

A current anthropogenous insult is likely to be at least as pervasive as the past ones, especially in New York. Acid rain, produced primarily by power generation, is effecting vegetational changes in the northeastern United States because it is more inimical to certain plant species than to others. Thus vegetational composition changes, and the natural climax is changed to a disclimax community. Since acid rain is a recent phenomenon and since many plants live so long, we know little about the exact trajectory of this vegetational change, but the effects are likely to be as drastic as those of lake acidification that have received so much public attention.

In addition to long-term effects of acid rain, other continuing modifications characterize the **Land Marks** site. Compared to the diurnal light cycle that challenged Monet at Rouen and Giverny, the cyclical and unidirectional changes facing **Land Marks** artists are enormous. There is daily light change, of course, and on this daily cycle is superimposed extreme seasonal change, so that the quality of dusk in winter is very different from that in summer. Since much of the vegetation is deciduous, the aspect of the site even aside from snow cover is drastically modified. The ravines appear to be near-climax communities, but the legacy of the historical factors discussed above has probably not yet exhausted itself, and the acid rain imposes a new succession on the entire site. Finally, the grassy portion has a number of "fairy rings," relics of underground fungi that will move from year to year as fungal spores disperse outward.

The Works

Certain of the submitted plans have strikingly captured ecological aspects of the site, while others, whatever their aesthetic merits, seem not closely tied to any particular location.

Athena Tacha's proposal is the most ambitious work conceptually, and unites many ecological aspects of the site in a complex metaphor for the relationship between humans and their environment. Observing on a topographic map that elevational isopleths of the ravines resemble a series of concentric oak leaves, she plans to accentuate this natural feature by terracing the grassy field into a set of nested oak leaves. The similarity of the isopleths to oak leaves is so apparent once noted that the overall scheme seems not the least contrived. Tacha imposes her own vision on this scheme, however. The terraces and all four leaves on her collage are leaves of white oak *(Quercus alba)*, with characteristic rounded lobes and indentations. The topographic isopleths, however, more nearly resemble species in the red oak subgenus, which have a jagged outline. There are many trees of two species in the red oak subgenus, northern red oak *(Quercus borealis)* and black oak *(Quercus velutina)*, in the surrounding ravines, and though white oak is most common, when I took twenty random samples of four oak leaves each from the **Land Marks** grounds, I always found at least one red or black oak among them.

The softer, more feminine outlines of the white oak leaves may be more condign to Tacha's essentially ameliorative message. She is warning humans that their technology can destroy nature and its symbol, the oak leaf. This destruction is expressed by eleven sets of steps, randomly strewn over the terraced leaves. Tacha's interest in steps as metaphors *(e.g.,* "Stepped Boogie-Woogie (Homage to Mondrian)" and "Dictionary of Steps") is manifested here particularly effectively. The terraces themselves are, of course, giant steps, while the smaller embedded steps she sees as representing, from the air, caterpillars feeding on an oak leaf, and, from a nearer vantage, vestiges of human activity left on the land. White oak leaves *are* attacked by a host of lepidopteran caterpillars eating from the outside and especially as leafminers within, between the two epithelial layers.[22] The steps *do,* in fact, resemble such caterpillars, and at least in the model, introduce the only note of destruction and decay into an otherwise vital and harmonious whole.

Caterpillars are, of course, normal constituents of the ecological community, and there is little evidence in most cases that white oaks are harmed in any way by them.[23] Furthermore, white oak is deciduous, and will drop its leaves each autumn whether or not they are damaged, though caterpillar feeding can accelerate this abscission. However, the other scale of destruction that Tacha's steps represent, the scars humans leave on the landscape, is rendered particularly insidious by her expansion of this scale from local to global: she embeds on the steps photographs and descriptions of the major accomplishments of science and technology, and of the threats these pose to nature and humankind. These threats constitute a series ranging from worldwide *(e.g.,* nuclear war) through regional *(e.g.,* acid rain) to local *(e.g.,* pollution of the Hudson River). The sample messages for the great cities theme (modern building technology *vs.* environmental pollution) and the rocketry theme (achievements of space technology *vs.* nuclear weapons) are well researched from a scientific standpoint and poetically assembled. These threats, and the way she has chosen to represent them, effectively symbolize a paradox inherent in all life, since the decrease in entropy effected by living organisms during reproduction and ontogeny must, by the laws of thermodynamics, entail an increase in entropy and disorder elsewhere in their environments. Schrodinger[24] thus termed life a temporary island of order in a sea of increasing entropy, and one readily understands this metaphor from the facts Tacha assembles on the "great cities" steps. The statistics of New York City's massive constructions like the Empire State Building and the Verrazano Narrows Bridge are juxtaposed with the statistics of accompanying waste and destruction—"New York City generates more than 70% of the sewage sludge dumped in the ocean," "the Hudson and East Rivers receive 250 million gallons of raw sewage per day," etc. The dominant message is depressing, since the dangers are all already upon us, but there is an undercurrent of hope. The sheer majesty of the depicted human accomplishments suggests the possibility of controlling the awesome destruction that has been unleashed, so that the loss of the giant oak leaves (nature) may be no more permanent than the loss of white oak leaves is each fall.

In sum, Tacha has transformed a number of features of the site into a series of metaphors, on several levels, for the relationship among nature, humankind, and technology. The metaphors are so interrelated, by use of the same physical constructs to symbolize several different forms of the same phenomenon, that the entire enterprise is endowed with a powerful aesthetic, ecological, and sociological unity.

Beatrice Perry's "Trans-12" also captures the ecological essence of the **Land Marks** site and uses it to probe the ways in which humans and their technology interact with nature. But Perry focusses on different site-specific traits than Tacha does, and the messages of the two artists, though formally similar in the statements accompanying their plans, are transmitted very differently. Perry's appeal is inferential; Tacha's is much more explicit. "Trans-12" is the largest of Perry's "Trans" series and like her other recent works *(e.g.,* "Sundance" and "China") uses massive sculpted steel sheets. This work is designed for a high, flat part of the triangle, and the sheer size of the piece (ca. 60′×84′) responds to the openness of the triangle and the size of the surrounding trees, especially the enormous white pines. To me, the contours of several of the steel plates were strikingly reminiscent of silhouettes of the imposing white pines along the triangular base; Perry also relates the contours to the mountains of the region. The size of the work, especially the height of the largest steel plates, combines with the surprising vistas that one sees through the corridors that suddenly open and close as one walks around "Trans-12" to introduce a brooding tension. This is not a comforting, womb-like nature, but a troubled one. Perry's statement shows that this tension is deliberate, and is additionally achieved by the specific juxtaposition of the different plates. Perry suggests that this tension may mirror our anxiety over the threat that industrial technology, represented by the steel forms and machinery used to shape them, presents to nature, represented by the site.

To me the anxiety is also partly induced by the inevitable changes, both natural and anthropogenous, that the site and thus its sculpture will undergo. "Trans-12" will have no base, and the soil dug up during its construction will be colonized by the herbs and shrubs that ensue during natural succession. In addition, the steel itself will undergo a progressive change from weathering. Also, the stainless steel reflects environmental colors—blue sky, spring and summer greenery, autumn reds and golds, and winter snow. One can easily imagine that the two stainless steel sheets will resemble, in these seasonal change, the surrounding mountains.

Finally, the massive steel forms set in the center of the raised cleared area resonate with the huge white pines along the triangular base to enhance the vaguely religious aura of the site. The initial view of "Trans-12" would have the same impact as the sudden appearance of the modern monolith to ancestral humans in Kubrick's "2001." Perry has produced an industrial Stonehenge, and the juxtaposition of the powerful centerpiece of quintessentially modern steel with the surrounding vegetation suggests a critical cleavage point: Technology can either harmonize with or destroy primordial nature, and "Trans-12" is a prayer for harmony.

Michael Singer's wooden longhouse is, in some ways, the antithesis of Perry's sculpture, yet addresses many of the same issues. It is intended for a wooded ravine rather than the high grassy area, and is a comforting rather than threatening evocation of human impact on nature. This work is squarely in Singer's neo-primitivist[25] tradition. Singer's site works are physically very close to undisturbed nature,[26] and the ravine forest is much further advanced successionally than is the rest of the site. The entire enterprise is vaguely womblike, with the closed house containing, on one side, several large stones set in rectangular holes in the earth, as if in gestation. This is a womb with a view, however, as the stones on the other side of the house are set above the ground, on wooden platforms, and communication between the inside of the construction and the forest is enhanced by portals and doorways, and by a roof open on one side. Whereas Perry's construction is of high technology steel, Singer, as in his previous work, uses only pre-Iron age materials—wood, dirt, stones. There is only harmony with nature, whereas in "Trans-12" the harmony coexists with tension. Nothing in this work suggests human threat to nature. Instead, it seems to reflect an early stage in a process by which *Homo sapiens* evolves with or is integrated into nature. The **Land Marks** piece perhaps represents a later stage in this evolution than does, *e.g.,* "Ritual Series." It is larger, more tightly constructed, and, by virtue of its walkways and rectangular openings, resembles traditional Japanese homes of the last century.

The work is inferential, as Perry's is, and its symbolism is subtle and susceptible to various interpretations. There is also, as in Perry's sculpture, a religious patina to this work. Its austere, clean lines and the large stones on platforms suggest, if not a temple or deity, at least an altar for a stylized ritual. But the ambiguity in the religiosity of "Trans-12," the recognition that the prayer may go unheeded, is absent from Singer's work. There is no hint here of potential discord between nature and humankind.

Despite the manifest interplay between Singer's longhouse and the surrounding forest, there is not a tight relationship between this work and its site, except for the topographic peculiarity of a deep ravine. There is no indication where the wood and stones are to come from, nor particular use of the surrounding vegetation. This construction would be equally effective in any forest, even one not near climax, in any region of great topographic relief. It could as well be set in the foothills of the Andes as in New York State. Its message is universal, but is not transmitted through attention to special features of the site.

Richard Fleischner's stone block construction is problematic in much the same way that Singer's building is. The incomplete walls and especially the arch constructed of up to four layers of massive pink-grey granite blocks connote the ruin of an ancient complex human construction. One can again imagine, because of the large blocks, the sheer size of the construction (its length is 32 feet), and the evocation of Stonehenge or of ruined Greek temples, a religious purpose. Because the work will be high (8 feet), irregular, and walls are incomplete, there will be different vistas as one walks around and through it, as with "Trans-12." Fleischner's previous concern with the relationship between shelter and enclosing spatial boundaries is continued here, and the shelter afforded by this work is comforting, if not so enveloping as that given by Singer's building. As with Singer's longhouse, the openings allow free communication between the interior of the construction and the site, and Fleischner has, like Singer, chosen a unique site for his work: *behind* the hedgerow that parallels the triangular base, with a smaller hedgerow to its side and the house near the triangular apex in clear view. Thus, the work will not be easily visible from the road in front of the Blum Gallery, or even from much of the grassy field.

I am curious about this carefully specified site; one might have expected the high area on the grass in front of the hedgerow, as a natural focus. Yet there is little about the work that seems specific to this site, on any scale, in spite of Fleischner's concern with detailed understanding of particular sites for his works.[27] The annotated topographic map provided to the artists indicates "natural field" for the region behind the long hedgerow, as opposed to "grass" in front of it, but this is an oxymoron, as a field in this region will succeed to forest without unnatural disturbance. The space behind the long hedgerow appeared to have similar herbs to those in front of it, but was not quite so well mown, and the herbs were interspersed with small shrubs in the vicinity of the smaller hedgerows. Thus the area is perhaps a later sucessional stage than is the grassy field, but not much later. I doubt that the exact composition of the ground cover matters to one's perception of the construction, so long as it be low. The building material, granite, is exotic, as bedrock in this region is sandstone and shale.[28] One can thus relate the exotic rock to the exotic plants in the hedgerows, and one can also relate the intrusive construction in this disturbed site to the intrusion of the house nearby. However, any unforested field sites with adjacent buildings would provide these characteristics, and the aesthetic qualities of the construction would probably be just as manifest in many of them.

Feigenbaum's "An Approximate Original Contour" terraces the field and parts of the ravines, and the terraces parallel the natural isopleths, but not so closely as in Tacha's plan. The terraces, by slightly inclining inward, will create rivulets for rain water that will be channeled to canals, which will ultimately drain into a lake and, eventually, into the Hudson River. This conception accentuates the linkage between the site and the Hudson, which is visually obscured by trees, and also calls attention to the unusual topography of the site and to the drainage pattern that one would normally take for granted.

That the resulting lake can be used as a skating rink is not surprising, as Feigenbaum's reclamation projects are functional as well as artistic. Feigenbaum specifies that natural existing vegetation is to be preserved in the ravines, so it is odd that the main tree species to be planted for both aesthetic purposes and windbreaks is the introduced Norway spruce. Plants for the terraces are indicated in very general terms—grasses, vines, etc. On the other hand, three native plants, one a threatened species, are suggested for the canal banks, and natural stone is to be used rather than concrete. "Contour" enhances and reflects aspects of the **Land Marks** site. It will undergo pronounced seasonal changes, as lake and skating rink alternate, and the ascent up the spiral terrace will present very different perspectives in summer and winter.

Jackie Ferrara's "Bard Platform" exploits just one trait of the **Land Marks** site, but exploits it so thoroughly that her project is intimately tied to this location. She continues to work on the border between sculpture and architecture, but does this more explicitly and on a larger scale than in her previous work. Once again she has constructed a wooden modified pyramid, but this one is 48′ by 30′8″ at its base. The ambiguity of scale and function[29] *(e.g.,* in "Kiosk") are gone; even without her statement, we would have been certain that the top is designed as a performance stage. This is a striking conception, as the location of "Bard Platform" in the high, grassy triangle extends the topographic isopleths to a magnificent conclusion. In the tile and concrete deck she adds a new material to her work, and extends the use of color that she introduced with "Grey Gazebo" in 1982. The colors (grey, green, and white) mirror and complement those of the site, and much of soil in the Bard region is clay. Similarly, the concrete could be viewed as related to the indigenous cement industry, founded on the clay, shale, and limestone in the region. However, the wood that comprises the greatest part of the work is designated as "cedar," of which there are about 17 species in eight genera. This would almost certainly be *Thuya gigantea,* Oregon red or white cedar. There are a few small *Juniperus virginiana* (pencil cedar or red cedar) in the hedgerow, but this species is not used for boards of the size required for "Bard Platform." Hence, the main material is allochthonous.

In addition to its performance function, Ferrara intends her work to be a changing visual experience as one ascends the platform. She stresses perception of the work itself *(e.g.,* the juxtaposition of the raised wooden platform and the ground level tile and concrete deck), but the ascent of six feet will also modify one's perception of the site, particularly by allowing one to see over the central hedgerow. Thus, especially in summer when deciduous vegetation has its leaves, climbing this work will afford a more comprehensive understanding of the work and its site.

Carolee Thea's "Daphne" can be construed, according to her text, as depicting the tension between nature and culture, simply because of its specific reference to the myth of Daphne and Apollo. It is much more than this, however. By virtue of the location of the statues, both deep in the ravine and along a large stretch of the road separating the ravines from the field, it must call attention to the topography and vegetation of the site, and, in particular, to the disclimax of the plateau relative to the later successional stages of the woods. The anguished Munch-like final statue, juxtaposed with the winter photographs of the deciduous vegetation, conveys a bleak message, as if Daphne's transformation into a tree is as much entrapment as escape. The same posture may seem incongruous in summer, however, when soft green surroundings would appear to welcome and shelter the nymph. Weeds that would obscure the pieces are to be trimmed, but would probably enhance the apparent progressive incorporation of Daphne into the forest, especially if allowed to colonize the base of the last statue. The fact that the statues form a sequence seems not to have been exploited to integrate the myth with the specific features of the site, or to explore more deeply the dichotomy that the myth addresses.

Sonfist's contribution is problematic. He continues to show a concern for succession and its site-specific qualities, but the **Land Marks** project simply mirrors the tower of leaves discussed above. Over several years, these leaves will come to produce, if not distinct strata, at least a gradient of decomposition from those that have formed humus at the bottom to the fresh leaves at the top. Sonfist has also been interested in soil strata; *e.g.,* in Atlanta he revealed the layers of earth beneath the city, with penetrating roots. The leaf tower will certainly expose hyphae of the decomposer fungi, and the deciduous vegetation will allow this piece to serve as an exemplar of soil succession. The site will create an illustration of itself, which will emphasize certain site-specific features.

"Still Pure Water" by Helen, Newton, and Joshua Harrison and Bettina Marks is a disappointment. There is nothing about this work that would prevent its construction in Indianapolis or Miami. Ecologically there is little of interest here, and this is surprising in light of the Harrisons' earlier treatment of succession. There is even a technical ecological problem that seems not to have been recognized. The aesthetic of this work is one of severe economy, almost sterility—it is "pure," "stainless," "anodized." Yet the glass and channel will surely be colonized by algae if clorox or some other impurity is not introduced. Aside from the visual effects of such colonists, the water will be contaminated by their activities and by whatever chemical is used to combat them.

Holt and Ross treat astronomical features of the **Land Marks** site. The nine circular buildings of Holt's "O Silo" include openings as locators, or else lines connecting the buildings themselves would indicate key directions. Locators mark the directions of sunrise and sunset at summer and winter solstices, and the compass directions. Those locators that lack openings can function because the 90-foot high central silo is topped by a viewing platform. Not only can one thus observe the compass directions and sun trajectories at points of greatest declination north and south of the celestial equator, but, since the entire project is destined for the high, grassy triangle, the river and mountains beyond will be visible. Furthermore, from 90 feet above ground, one will have a much better sense of the steep ravines and thus the platform nature of the triangle will be enhanced. "O Silo" will capture the seasonal change of the site explicitly by depicting the relation of sun and earth, rather than by focussing on the vegetation that is our more usual cue.

Ross incorporates his continuing interests in the changing celestial map and compound nature of sunlight into "When the Stars Speak Shape." His construction is shaped by the position of the **Land Marks** site on the surface of the earth and the position and inclination of the earth relative to stars. A concrete "solar disk" is set perpendicular to the sun's rays at equinoctial noon. A small prism is mounted in a slot in the disk so that a spectrum crosses the chamber formed by the disk and its frame, a vivid demonstration of the earth's rotation. An observer standing on a "viewing stone" some distance from the disk, and sighting in a line with the prism slot, will face the star Polaris, the celestial pole. But the relative positions and movements of earth and Polaris cause the star to appear to move in a circle as time passes. The largest of Polaris's apparent orbits will not occur again until about 15,000 A.D., while the smallest will next occur about a century from now. Ross has shaped the frame over which the viewer sees Polaris so that it is an arc of two concentric circles; the larger one is part of Polaris's largest orbit. The smaller one is part of the daily orbit of the pole of the ecliptic. The ecliptic is the great circle on the celestial sphere that forms the apparent path of the sun over the course of the year. The slight apparent daily movement of the ecliptic causes its pole to have a circular orbit, and it is a part of this circle that Ross has used in his frame. Changes on time scales from days through millennia are thus demonstrated. The orientation, size, and shape of the construction that demonstrates these changes depend completely on the geography and topography of the site.

Holt and Ross have thus called attention to site characteristics on a larger and longer scale than ecologists normally treat. Though they could have produced analogous works for any location, their conceptions and interests are especially well suited to the **Land Marks** site because of its raised plateau and latent religiosity. Ross's work is a sort of altar; the celestial mechanics that govern his shapes impose themselves forcefully on this site. It is as if one is at the top of the world. One would expect star worshippers to revere this location. The same clear yet elevated property gives Holt's high silo a dominating quality it would not easily achieve elsewhere, even atop a mountain, and her use of the solstices, which have roles in several religions, invests her work with an aura of worship.

Some of the submitted plans are for exciting projects, but do not seem especially related to the **Land Marks** site. Robert Morris's "Bard Project" is tangentially related to site art as I have traced its phylogeny, but not to Bard. The siting instructions—"To be placed in an open field"—confirm that the details of the site, and even its regional location, are unimportant. This is a compelling piece, and certainly responds to the **Land Marks** charge of exploring the relationship among humans, nature, and society. Morris's continuing obsession with the threat of nuclear annihilation finds chilling expression in the series of huge, progressively more ominous, phallic missile-like cylinders. The sequence from stone through bronze to steel implies an inevitable development and deployment of the capacity for societal destruction. The apparently harmless beginning—emergence of stone from an earth berm—engages nature as part of the conception, but the bronze and steel cylinders, with their awful connotation, submerge nature and focus quite exclusively on humankind. The sexual metaphor for missiles has been well explored in literature *(e.g.,* Thomas Pynchon's *Gravity's Rainbow*[30]), but is nowhere so graphic as in "Bard Project." I take Morris's use of the metaphor to enhance the natural or evolutionary aspects of the rush to self-annihilation, but one could as well interpret it more complexly—for example, the order-building process of reproduction necessarily, by the laws of thermodynamics, entailing and feeding on death and destruction as I discussed in connection with Tacha's contribution. Such a rendering is, of course far more elusive for a visual artist than for a writer, and Tacha's transmission of this theme was by written messages on her steps.

Dennis Oppenheim's four plans are even less related to the **Land Marks** site or to site art *per se.* Although each plan includes specific suggestions for siting, the required features (openness, slope, near a building, etc.) are not peculiar to Bard College. Nor, except for "Roots in Cubism. Hearts in the Stars. (Forest for Cezanne)," is the site or land in general an integral part of these planned works. The other three projects are typical Oppenheim contraptions, each with either implied or actual movement and a wealth of unusual materials welded into dynamic entities that demand attention.

"Roots in Cubism" is another matter—frankly stationary and, because it depicts the interaction of trees and the human mind, necessarily located near trees. The size of the work is intended to match the size of the trees. The relationship between "Roots in Cubism" and the **Land Marks** trees is superficial, however, particularly since Oppenheim intends it to represent Cezanne's abstraction of the geometric essence of trees. The geometries of different tree species are strikingly different, responding to the selective pressures of their different environments and ecological strategies.[31] These differences are readily apparent to artists. For example, European artists had great difficulty depicting the very different trees and forests of the newly discovered Pacific islands, including Australia, in the 18th and 19th centuries, and these exotic shapes came to influence European conceptions of the relationship between man and nature.[32] Similarly, the huge white pines that dominate one suggested site (#12) differ so greatly from the hedgerow trees, primarily deciduous, in the vicinity of the other site (#5) that any geometric abstraction of the former could not possibly represent the latter. The pines are enormous, stately, relatively sparse and narrow, with few horizontal branches springing from a majestic trunk. The trees near site #5 are either shrubby or else have a relatively short trunk and dense spherical crown. Some have multiple trunks, through either suckering *(e.g.,* red cedar) or clonal growth *(e.g.,* dogwoods and sumacs). They are in no sense majestic or foreboding, as the pines are; instead, their scale is human and they are comforting or sheltering. Yet, except for size, there are no planned differences for constructions of the project at the two potential locations. Even aspects of size are invariable—the tree trunk, for example, will always be 4.5 feet in diameter.

Jody Pinto's three plans are similarly not intimately related to the **Land Marks** site. The stated connotations for the two plans that use a Catherine wheel suggest the wheel as an exploded metaphor for the relationship of humans to technology, but the interaction of nature with humans and their machines is more subtly addressed. It is an evolutionary commonplace that among all of the machine analogs (hearts as pumps, limbs as levers, etc.) that nature has produced, the wheel is conspicuously absent, yet I doubt if Pinto's wheels can be viewed as an abrupt break from nature. They are to be seeded (though the type of seed is unspecified) and she envisions unnamed plants as growing in the cement block interstices, so there is some accommodation of human structures to ecological succession. Although she does not mention it, the main ecological changes would be that variously shaped and colored lichens would colonize the blocks, in random and striking patterns. The axel tower associated with one of the wheels, as well as the "Tower for the Study of Languages," both are intended for the highest part of the triangle and seem appropriate for the topography of the site, as I have discussed above, but little else is site-specific. The listed connotations for the second tower have similar impact as those for the Catherine wheel, with the striking exception of the juxtaposition of "split tongue," "loss of speech," and "speech—the capacity that defines us as sovereign over nature." Since the tower is also to be seeded and to have grasses in its interstices, and will again be colonized by lichens, it can symbolize our inability to dominate nature, but the "nature" is a generalized conception, not the particular nature that will surround the tower.

Aycock's "A Representation of the Second World" and Stuart's "The Bard's Song Book" seem unrelated to the **Land Marks** site.

Ana Mendieta's art has never, as she writes in her supporting text, fit comfortably into the mainstream of site art. Although she senses that her work has evolved in response to characteristics of different landscapes, individual works do not manifest specific relationships to their sites; this is true of "La Maja de Yerba," planned for **Land Marks.** As do her previous earthworks, "La Maja de Yerba" renders a female form on the surface of the earth. The proposed permanence of this work sets it apart from earlier ones *(e.g.,* "The Vivification of the Flesh") that were intended only as subjects for photographs. Consequently, the raised earthen mound forming the outline is to be planted, but with an introduced English grass, *"Racrostes."* The explicitly sexual female form celebrates the fertility of nature, as well as the fact that humans are part of nature and the location at the highest point of the site emphasizes the incantory mode of Mendieta's rendering, as if nature is appealing to its creator. I sense that "La Maja de Yerba" would be a powerful construction, but there are internal contradictions that are troubling. I am unable to locate *"Racrostes"* in standard botanical dictionaries, but I suspect from her description that Mendieta intends colonial bentgrass *(Agrostis tenuis)* to be planted. This exotic species, which has an artificial, rug-like quality, evokes the garden of "unnatural," "synthetic" plants in *A Rebours,* while the continued trimming that would be required to maintain it would render the piece an artificial disclimax. A bounty of nature is to be stemmed rather than expressed. A strangely sterile piece will represent the fertility of nature.

Cecile Abish's contribution is one of the most expansive in **Land Marks,** and would occupy the entire plateau. Her architectural and urban planning background is apparent, as the work consists of a large deck (of introduced cedar, *Thuya gigantea,* the same wood specified by Ferrara) for observing a formal park, which will have elaborate brick walls and portals as well as planted lawns and forests. Rather than encompass the site and its vegetation as an integral feature, this work would obliterate the original traits of this site by excavation, clearcutting, construction, and planting. Geometric features, such as the parallel elements in the deck, walls, and gravel pathway, would be most apparent from the air, as the deck will be low (4.5 feet) and the walls high (6.5 feet). This is a far cry from the low-lying earthworks that she first produced. The aesthetic for this work is as much in the realm of topiary as in that of earth art, and I would argue that it is not site art *sensu stricto.* From the drawing and description I get the impression that it would be most effective in an urban setting; in any event, I see no special relation to the Bard site.

Discussion

A pervasive and surprising aspect of most **Land Marks** works is that they are not very sensitive to the vegetation that combines with the topography to give the site its unique character. Approximately half the artists make no mention of vegetation in discussions of construction, maintenance, and materials. The remainder almost all speak in very general terms—"grass or ground cover," "tall grass," "trees," "vines," "weeds," "lawn," etc. Few species are specified for planting, and two of these are not found in the region. Tacha and Perry alone have exploited the site vegetation, the latter by the evocative resonance between the steel plates and white pines, the former by recognizing the dominance of oaks and the coincidental relationship between oaks and the topography.

It is probably not coincidental that Perry is the only resident of the **Land Marks** region. Natives are much more sensitive than are casual visitors to the subtle differences among members of a local biota. Mayr[33] gives a striking example:

> If one studies the birds, the mammals, the butterflies, or the snails near his home town, he finds each species clearly defined and sharply separated from all other species. This is sometimes better appreciated by primitive natives than by modern civilized man. Some 30 years ago I spent several months with a tribe of superb woodsmen and hunters in the Arfak Mountains of New Guinea. They had 136 different vernacular names for the 137 species of birds that occurred in the area, confusing only two species.

For another example, the Tzeltal Indians of Chiapas, Mexico, have 471 names for plant species, of which 61% correspond to Linnaean names.[34] Most errors consist of lumping together species that are very similar morphologically. On the other hand, the bottle gourd *(Lagenaria siceraria),* a heavily used species, is split into several species corresponding to different uses made of different sized gourds. No Tzeltal would simply say "vine" or "weed" or "tree."

The natives of the New Guinean and Mexican highlands live in much more intimate interdependence with unmodified nature than we do, so one might expect them to be very good at differentiating species—their very lives may rest on this ability. Systematists also should be very sensitive to species differences—their *modus operandi* is to deploy many technologies to detect elusive differences between species that may be remarkably similar morphologically. Site artists may similarly sense subtle properties that distinguish one species from another, especially if they are engaging the site as part of an aesthetic conception, as I have claimed. Such distinctions are not casual matters, however, for aborigines, taxonomists, or aesthetes. Whatever inborn sensitivities infuse an artist's perceptions, if these are to aid in understanding and rendering the complexities of ecological communities they must be leavened with intense familiarity with biotic and abiotic features.

It also surprised me that so little attention was paid to other components of the ambient biota that often come to dominate the appearance of all but the largest earthworks. Lichens of many colors cover most surfaces—especially stone—as they cover trees in the Bard region, though air pollution may make them less dominant. Algae colonize almost any surface usually covered with water. Any isolated statue in a field is likely to be festooned with guano, and the hieroglyphic trails left by their radulae as snails graze many surfaces are often striking. Yet site artists have not explored these traits much more than did artists placing their works outdoors in centuries past; **Land Marks** is no exception.

I am not demanding that every site work be cognizant of every biotic element in its surroundings. Ecologists are often blithely uninterested in pervasive organisms, like nematodes and mites. Rather, I mean to point out that site artists have barely exploited the potential that most sites have for expressing ideas and aesthetic impulses. It also seems to me that the intellectual demands that site art places on its practitioners exceed those of any other art form, simply by virtue of the complexity of most sites. Just as detailed knowledge of musculature and articulation enhances representation of animal forms, intensive understanding of the structure and function of natural communities certainly deepens a work's resonance with its site. Yet even a barren site such as a desert is vastly more complex than is an individual organism. If it is not really a superorganism, an ecosystem and its community nonetheless have interactions and organization of many types. Of course it may be possible to sense or intuit aspects of a site much as a painter may abstract elements of a scene. But the fact that site art is embedded in the scene allows considerably more scope for abstraction and integration. It is inconceivable, however, that the entire essence of a site can be grasped without lengthy and rather formal study, Holt's attempt[35] notwithstanding. Perhaps site art is even more in its infancy than ecology is, and its full development will require artists who are scientists as well as aesthetes.

Acknowledgements

I am grateful to Linda Weintraub, Erik Kiviat, and Mary Tebo for advice and discussion on various aspects of this essay.

References

[1]Adcock, C. 1983(April). "The big bad: A critical comparison of Mount Rushmore and modern earthworks." *Arts* 57(April 1983):104-107.
[2]Castle, T. "Nancy Holt, siteseer." *Art in America* 70(March 1982):84-91.
[3]Beardsley, J. *Probing the Earth: Contemporary Land Projects.* Washington, D.C.: Smithsonian Institution Press, 1977.
[4]Ibid.
[5]Simberloff, D. 1980. "A succession of paradigms in ecology: Essentialism to materialism and probabilism." *Synthesis* 42(1980):3-39.
[6]Egerton, F. "Changing Concepts on the Balance of Nature." *Quarterly Review of Biology* No. 2, June 1973:332-350
[7]Simberloff, op.cit.
[8]Raup, H. 1981. *Forests in the Here and Now.* Missoula, Mont.: Montana Forest and Conservation Experiment Station, School of Forestry, University of Montana, 1986.
[9]Ibid.
[10]Castle, op.cit.
[11]Foote, N. "Situation esthetics." *Artforum* 18(Jan. 1980):22-29.
[12]Simberloff, op.cit.
[13]Ibid.
[14]Simberloff, D. "Entropy, Information, and Life: Biophysics in the Novels of Thomas Pynchon." *Perspectives in Biology and Medicine,* Volume 21, Number 4, Summer 1978: 577-625.
[15]Ibid.
[16]West, D.C., H.H. Shugart, and D.B. Botkin (eds.). *Forest Succession: Concepts and Applications.* New York:Springer, 1981.
[17]Kiviat, E. *Hudson River East Bank Natural Areas, Clermont to Norrie.* Arlington, Va.: The Nature Conservancy, 1978.
[18]Ibid.
[19]Lippard, L., "Gardens: Some Metaphors for a Public Art." *Art in America* 69(Nov. 1981):148.
[20]Cairns, J., Dickson, K.L., Kerricks, E.E., *Proceedings of the International Symposium on the Recovery of Damaged Ecosystems,* 1975:Recovery and Restoration of Damaged Ecosystems. Charlottesville:University Press of Virginia, 1977.
[21]Kiviat, op.cit.
[22]Connor, E.F., S.H. Faeth, and D. Simberloff. "Leafminers on Oaks: The Role of Immigration and in situ Reproductive Recruitment. *Ecology,* Volume 64, No. 1(1983):191-204.
[23]Ibid.
[24]Schrodinger, E. *What Is Life? And Other Scientific Essays.* Garden City, N.Y., Doubleday, 1956.
[25]Kuspit, D.B. "Caves and temples." *Art in America,* 69(April 1982):129-133.
[26]Feinberg, J.E. "Michael Singer: Ritual series." *Arts* 57(June 1983):69-73.
[27]Onorato, R.J. "Richard Fleischner's Baltimore project." *Arts* 56(Oct. 1981):64-67.
[28]Kiviat, op.cit.
[29]Heartney, E. 1983(March). Jackie Ferrara. *Arts* 57:9.
[30]Simberloff, *Entropy, Information, and Life,* op.cit.
[31]Horn, H.S. *The Adaptive Geometry of Trees.* Princeton, New Jersey:Princeton University Press, 1971. Halle, F., R.A.A. Oldeman, and P.B. Tomlinson. *Tropical Trees and Forests: An Architectural Analysis.* Berlin:Springer, 1978.
[32]Smith, Bernard. 1969. *European Vision and the Discovery of the South Pacific, 1768-1850: A Study in the History of Art and Ideas.* Sydney:Oxford University Press, 1969.
[33]Mayr, E. *Animal Species and Evolution.* Cambridge, Massachusetts:Harvard, 1963.
[34]Berlin, B., D.E. Breedlove, and P.H. Raven. 1966. "Folk taxonomies and biological classification." *Science* 154(1966):273-275.
[35]Castle, op.cit.

ARTISTS' BIOGRAPHIES

Cecile Abish

Born: New York, NY
Education: BFA, Brooklyn College
Selected Outdoor Sculpture Projects:
"Renaissance Fix Project Series/Piedmont Park," Atlanta, GA, 1980
"Shifting Concern," New Brunswick, NJ, 1975
"Sculpture-In-The-Park," Paramus, NJ, 1974
"Burning Blue," Stuttgart, West Germany, 1974, 1981
"4 Into 3," Mahwah, NJ, 1973
"Field Quartering," Peoria, IL, 1972
"Aldrich East Kraft Paper Field," Ridgefield, CT, 1971
"Upside Down Sienna Field," New York, NY, 1971

Alice Aycock

Born: Harrisburg, PA
Education: BA, Douglass College, MA, Hunter College
Selected Outdoor Sculpture Projects:
"100 Small Rooms," Houston, TX, 1984
"The Leonardo Swirl II," Antwerpen, Belgium, 1983
"The Solar Wind" From the Series Entitled: "A Theory of Universal Causality (Time/Creation Machines)," Salem, VA, 1983
"The Miraculating Machine in the Garden (Tower of the Winds)," New Brunswick, NJ, 1982
"The Large Scale Dis/Integration of Micro-Electronic Memories," Battery Park, NY, 1980
"The Game of Fliers," Washington, D.C., 1980
"On the Eve of the Industrial Revolution, A City Engaged in the Production of False Miracles," Bloomfield Hills, MI, 1978
"The Beginnings of a Complex . . .: Excerpt Shaft #4/Five Walls," Artpark, Lewiston, NY, 1977
"The Beginnings of a Complex . . .: Documenta," Kassel, Germany, 1977
"Heavy Roofed Building," Los Angeles, CA, 1976
"Wooden Posts Surrounded by Fire Pits," Roslyn, NY, 1976
"Wooden Shacks on Stilts with Platform," West Hartford, CT, 1976
"Circular Building With Narrow Ledges for Walking," Silver Springs, PA, 1976
"Simple Network of Underground Wells and Tunnels," Far Hills, NJ, 1975
"Williams College Project," Williamstown, MA, 1974
"Walled Trench/Earth Platform/Center Pit," New Kingston, PA, 1974
"Low Building With Dirt Roof (For Mary)," New Kingston, PA, 1973
"Maze," New Kingston, PA, 1972
"Sun/Glass," Silver Springs, PA, 1971

Agnes Denes

Born: Budapest, Hungary
Education: CUNY, New School for Social Research, Columbia University
Selected Outdoor Sculpture Projects:
"Wheatfield," Battery Park City, NY, NY, 1982
"Rice/Tree/Burial Project," Artpark, Lewiston, NY, 1979
"Time/Fuse/Attitudes," Bulderup, Sweden, 1979
"Time Capsule," Artpark, Lewiston, NY, 1977
"Haiku Poetry Burial, Rice Planting and Tree Chaining," Sullivan County, NY, 1968

Harriet Feigenbaum

Born: New York, NY
Education: Art Students League, National Academy of Design, Columbia University
Selected Outdoor Sculpture Projects:
"Last Rites at Lands End," Orchard Beach, NY, 1985
"Stones, Trees, Water and Light for a Mid-Summer Evening," New York, NY, 1984
"Reclamation of Strip Mine Spoils," The Storrs, Dickson City, PA: "Valley of 8000 Pines," 1983, "Black Walnut Forest," 1984, "Serpentine Vineyard," 1985
"Transformations to an Inner Island Village," Ward's Island, NY, 1978-80
"Battery Park City—A Mirage," New York, NY, 1978
"Parking Lot Pentagon Off Washington Avenue," 1978, Brooklyn, NY, 1978
"Land Structures Built Where the Petroglyphs Are Made By Children," Artpark, Lewiston, NY, 1977
"The Structuring of Barren Ground," Greve, Italy, 1976
"Cycles," Roslyn, NY, 1976
"Tuscan Valley Configuration of Hay and Wood," New York, NY, 1976
"Hayricks Until August Fires," Torre al Pino, Molino del Piano, Italy, 1974
"The Haying Process," Far Hills, NJ, 1974
"Windricks in the Mistral at Mas de S. Jerone," Maussane, France, 1973
"The Haying Process—Hay Constructions," New York, NY, 1972
"Hay Structures on the Farm of Duke and Dutchess Salviati," Migliarino Pisano, Italy, 1971
"The Gates of Cinaglio," Cinaglio, Italy, 1969

Jackie Ferrara

Born: Detroit, MI
Education: Michigan State University
Selected Outdoor Sculpture Projects:
"A246 Breaktower," Columbus, OH, 1984
"A120 Stacked Pyramid," Purchase, NY, 1982
"A216 Laumeier Project," St. Louis, MO, 1981
"A206 Carbondale Project," Carbondale, IL, 1980
"A205 Wave Hill Project," Riverdale, NY, 1980
"A198 Castle Clinton Tower & Bridge," Battery Park, NY, 1979
"A195 Dayton Arch," Dayton, OH, 1978
"A192 Minneapolis Project," Minneapolis, MN, 1978
"A172 Trisected to Quartered Pyramid," New York, NY, 1976
"A120 Stacked Pyramid," New York, NY, 1976
"A120 Stacked Pyramid," Mountainville, NY, 1973

Richard Fleischner

Born: New York, NY
Education: BFA, MFA, Rhode Island School of Design
Selected Outdoor Sculpture Projects:
"Baltimore Project," Woodlawn, MD, 1980
"Fence Covered Fence," Lake Placid, NY, 1980
"Wood Interior," Providence, RI, 1980
"Sites Resited," Dayton, OH, 1978-79
"Chain Link Maze," Amherst, MA, 1978-79
"Floating Square," Kassel, West Germany, 1977
"Cow Island Project," Providence, RI, 1976-77
"Sod Construction," New York, NY, 1976
"Sited Works," Roslyn, NY, 1976
"Wood Interior," Artpark, Lewiston, NY, 1976
"Sod Drawing," Greenwich, CT, 1976
"Sod Drawing," Far Hills, NJ, 1975
"Sod Maze," Newport, RI, 1974
"Tufa Maze," Pocantico Hills, NY, 1973
"Zig Zag," Rehoboth, MA, 1972
"Bluff," Rehoboth, MA, 1972
"Hay Interior," Rehoboth, MA, 1971
"Hay Maze," Rehoboth, MA, 1971
"Incomplete Hay Square," Rehoboth, MA, 1971
"Hay Line," Rehoboth, MA, 1971
"Diner," Barrington, RI, 1966-68

Helen and Newton Harrison

Born: (Helen) New York, NY
(Newton) New York, NY
Education: (Helen) BA, Queens College, MA, Cornell University
(Newton) BFA, MFA, Yale University
Selected Outdoor Sculpture Projects:
"Baltimore Promenade," Baltimore, MD, 1981 (Helen and Newton Harrison)
"Spoils Pile Reclamation," Artpark, Lewiston, NY, 1977-78 (Helen, Newton and Joshua Harrison)
"The Third Lagoon," Hollywood Hills, CA, 1973-74 (Helen and Newton Harrison)
"Notations on the Eco-System of the Western Salt Works With the Inclusion of Brine Shrimp," Los Angeles, CA, 1971
"Bridge," San Diego, CA, 1969 (Newton Harrison)

Nancy Holt

Born: Worcester, MA
Education: BS, Tufts University
Selected Outdoor Sculpture Projects:
"Astral Grating," New York, NY, 1983-
"Waterwork," Washington, D.C., 1983-
"Sole Source," Dublin, Ireland, 1983
"Catch Basin," Toronto, Canada, 1982
"Time Span," Austin, TX, 1981
"Annual Ring," Saginaw, MI, 1980-81
"Rosslyn Park Project," Arlington, VA, 1979-
"Inside Out (Washington, D.C. NW)," Washington, D.C., n.d.
"Wild Spot," Wellesley, MA, 1979-80
"30 Below," Lake Placid, NY, 1979
"Star Crossed," Oxford, OH, 1979-80
"Polar Circle," Oxford, OH, 1979
"Stone Enclosure: Rock Rings," Bellingham, MA, 1977-78
"Sun Tunnels," Lucin, UT, 1973-76
"Hydra's Head," Lewiston, NY, 1974
"Missoula Ranch Locators," Missoula, MT, 1972
"Views Through a Sand Dune," Narragansett Beach, RI, 1972
"Buried Poems," FL, NJ, UT, 1969-71

Ana Mendieta

Born: Havana, Cuba
Education: MA, MFA, University of Iowa
Selected Outdoor Sculpture Projects:
"Furrows," Providence, RI, 1984
"Iberian Sculptures," Miami Beach, FL, 1983
"4 Elements Figures," Sag Harbor, NY, 1983
"Rio Grande Sculpture," Albuquerque, NM, 1982
"4 Sculptures," Miami, FL, 1982
"Labyrinth Figure," Toronto, Canada, 1982
"Arbitra," Hartford, CT, 1982
"Ceiba Fetish," Miami, FL, 1981
"Sculpture for the Ocean," Miami, FL, 1981
"Quarry Figure," Alfred, NY, 1981
"Ropestrian Sculptures," Havana, Cuba, 1981
"Tree/Figure," Ward's Island, NY, 1981
"Gunpowder Sculpture," Medellin, Columbia, 1981
"Mound," Medellin, Columbia, 1981
"Sculpture for a Cemetery," Washington, D.C., 1981
"Gunpowder Silhouette," New York, NY, 1980
"Cerro Figures," Oaxaca, Mexico, 1980
"Two Sculptures," Union, NJ, 1980
"Plakat Aktion," Frankfurt, Germany, 1980

Mary Miss

Born: New York, NY
Education: BA, University of California, MFA, Maryland Institute
Selected Outdoor Sculpture Projects:
"Untitled," Laumeier Sculpture Park, St. Louis, MO, 1984
"Field Rotation," Park Forest South, IL, 1981
"Veiled Landscape," Lake Placid, NY, 1979
"Staged Gates," Dayton, OH, 1979
"Blind Set," Artpark, Lewiston, NY, 1976
"Sunken Pool," Greenwich, CT, 1974
"Untitled," Battery Park City, NY, 1973
"Untitled," Oberlin, OH, 1973
"Ropes/Shore," Ward Island, NY, 1969
"Vs in the Field," Liberty Corner, NJ, 1969
"Window in Hill," Colorado Springs, CO, 1968
"Stakes and Ropes," Colorado Springs, CO, 1968

Robert Morris

Born: Kansas City, MO
Education: University of Kansas, Kansas City Art Institute, California School of Fine Arts, Reed College, MFA, Hunter College
Selected Outdoor Sculpture Projects:
Untitled, Documenta 6, Kassel,Germany, 1977
"Observatory," Oostelijk Flevoland, The Netherlands, 1977
"Labyrinth," University of Pennsylvania, Philadelphia, PA, 1974

"Grand Rapids Project," Grand Rapids, MI, 1973-74
Untitled (Steam Piece), University of Washington, Bellingham, WA, 1973
"Observatory," Santpoort/Velsen, The Netherlands, 1971, For "Sonsbeek 71," 1971

Dennis Oppenheim

Born: Electric City, WA
Education: BFA, California School of Arts and Crafts, MFA, Stanford University
Selected Outdoor Sculpture Projects:
"Roots in Cubism. Hearts in the Stars (Forest for Cezanne)," West Berlin, Germany, 1984
"Formula Compound. A Combustion Chamber. An Exorcism. (From the Fireworks Series)," SUNY Potsdam, NY, 1983-84
"Dreams and Nightmares. Journey of a Broken Weave," University of Albuquerque, NM, 1983
"Image Intervention," Anchorage, AK, 1983
"Formula Compound. A Combustion Chamber. An Exorcism," Pistoia, Italy, 1982-83
"Station for Detaining and Blinding Radio-Active Horses," Otterlo, Holland, 1982
"An Operation for Mining, Elevating and Converting Underground Memories of a Fifth Season," Bloomfield Hills, MI, 1980-81

Beatrice Perry

Born: Evanston, IL
Education: Art Institute of Chicago, Skidmore College, University of Chicago
Selected Outdoor Sculpture Projects:
"Water Sculpture," Sneeden's Landing, NY, 1983
"Water Sculpture," Munster, IN, 1983
"Trans IX," Greenwich, CT, 1982
"Trans VI," Las Vegas, NE, 1981
"Trans V," Highland Park, IL, 1978
"Trans IV," Annandale-on-Hudson, NY, 1977
"Outdoor Water Sculpture," Winnetka, IL, 1977
"Waterfall," West New York, NJ, 1976
"Trans III," Aspen, CO, 1976
"Trans II," Brooklyn, NY, 1975
"Trans I," Kalamazoo, MI, 1974

Jody Pinto

Born: New York, NY
Education: Pennsylvania Academy of the Fine Arts, BFA, Philadelphia College of Art
Selected Outdoor Sculpture Projects:
"Maumee Comet," Toledo, OH, 1983
"Finger Span: For Climbers Rock," Philadelphia, PA, 1983
"Springboard Chamber (for Icarus): a Device for a High Flying Dive," Sacramento, CA, 1982
"Widow's Perch," New York, NY, 1982
"Colorado Corridor," Boulder, CO, 1982
"Seeded Catherine Wheel," Kutztown, PA, 1982
"Project for the Origin of Ohio," Pittsburgh, PA, 1981
"Channel House for a Split-Tongue Pier," Philadelphia, PA, 1981
"Split-Tongue Pier," Swarthmore, PA, 1980
"Seeded Sight Wall," Upper Galilee, Israel, 1980
"Serpentine Corridor," Wooster, OH, 1980
"Flood Piece," Norman, OK, 1980
"Heart Chamber for Gertrude and Angelo," Philadelphia, PA, 1978
"Underground Chamber," Long Island City, NY, 1977
"Three Open Wells," Dayton, OH, 1977
"Penndot Landfill" (3 works), Philadelphia, PA, Montauk Point, NY, 1976
"Penndot Landfill" (5 works), Philadelphia, PA, Artpark, Lewiston, NY, 1975
"Wildlife Preserve," Cape May, NJ, 1974

Charles Ross

Born: Philadelphia, PA
Education: AB, MA, University of California, Berkeley
Selected Outdoor Sculpture Projects:*
"Rock Bow," O'Hare Rapid Transit, Chicago, IL, 1983
"West Light," Towson, MD, 1983
"Toward Seven," Grand Rapids, MI, 1982
Spectrum Building, Denver, CO, 1980
Dietrich Foundation, Philadelphia, PA, 1979
Prestonwood Town Center, Dallas, TX, 1979
"Two Prisms from the Origin of Color," Philadelphia, PA, 1977

*All works occur within a structure beneath a skylight

Michael Singer

Born: Brooklyn, NY
Education: BFA, Cornell University, Rutgers University, Yale University Norfolk Program
Selected Outdoor Sculpture Projects:
"First Gate Ritual Series 479," Dayton, OH, 1979
"Sangam Ritual Series 476," Edgewater, MD, 1976
"Ritual Series 775," Bear Mountain, NY 1975
"Lily Pond Ritual Series," Bear Mountain, NY, 1975
"Glades Ritual Series," Homestead, FL, 1975
"Marsh Ritual Series," Heckscher, NY, 1973

Alan Sonfist

Born: New York, NY
Education: MA, Hunter College, 1969
Selected Outdoor Sculpture Projects:
"Time Enclosers of the Southeast," Grove Isle, FL, 1975
"Crystal Monument," Dayton, OH, Corp. Ponderosa, Inc., 1972
"Columns of Growth," J.B. Speed Museum, Louisville, KY, 1979
"Rising Sun Monument," Temple University, Philadelphia, PA, 1980
"Sun Monument," University of Rhode Island, Kingston, RI, 1973
"Rising Washington Monument," Presidents Mall, Washington, D.C., 1984
"Rock Monument of Buffalo," Albright-Knox Museum, Buffalo, NY, 1965-78

"Time Landscape Dual History Forest," Mall, St. Louis, MO, 1965-78
"Time Landscape, Oak Forest," Greenwich Village, NY, 1965-78
"Time Landscape, Beach," Red Hook, Brooklyn, NY, 1965-78
"Time Landscape, Hemlock Hill," Marble Hill, NY, 1965-78

Robert Stackhouse

Born: Bronxville, NY
Education: BA, University of South Florida, MA, University of Maryland
Selected Outdoor Sculpture Projects:
"On the Beach Again," Canberra, Australia, 1984
"Red Deck," Chicago Navy Pier, Chicago, IL, 1983
"Bones," Portland, OR, 1983
"Toronto Passages," Ontario, Canada, 1982
"Passings at the Nassau County Museum," NY, 1980
"China Clipper," Indianapolis, IN, 1980
"Eau Claire Sailings," Eau Claire, WI, 1979
"Cranbrook Dance," Bloomfield Hills, MI, 1978
"Sailings at the Hudson River Museum," Yonkers, NY, 1978
"Ship at St. Agnes," Cleveland, OH, 1977
"Niagara Dance," Artpark, Lewiston, NY, 1977

Michelle Stuart

Born: Los Angeles, CA
Education: Chouinard Art Institute, New School for Social Research
Selected Outdoor Sculpture Projects:
"Sacred Precincts: Nantucket Excavation," Nantucket Island, MA, 1984
"Stone Alignments/Solstice Cairns," Rowena Plateau, Columbia River Gorge, OR, 1979
"Color/Time/Landform Transformations," Tomkins Cove Quarry, Stoney Point, NY, 1977
"Niagara Gorge Path Relocated," Artpark, Lewiston, NY, 1975

Athena Tacha

Born: Larissa, Greece
Education: MA, National Academy of Fine Arts, Athens, Greece, MA, Oberlin College, PhD, University of Paris
Selected Outdoor Sculpture Projects:
"Crossings," Columbus, OH, 1982
"Blair Fountain," Tulsa, OK, 1981-82
"Leaning Arches," Miami, FL, 1980-82
"Stepped Boogie-Woogie (Homage to Mondrian)," Seattle, WA, 1981-82
"Curving Arcades (Home to Bernini)," Tucson, AZ, 1980-81
"Twist," Cleveland, OH, 1980-81
"Perspective Arcade (Homage to Borromini)," Toledo, OH, 1979-80
"Ripples," Norfolk, VA, 1979
"Tide Park," Smithtown, NY, 1976-77
"Double Tension Arches," Columbus, OH, 1975-76
"Streams," Oberlin, OH, 1975-76
"Tension Arches," Cleveland, OH, 1975-76

Carolee Thea

Born: Brooklyn, NY
Education: MA, Hunter College, BA, Columbia University
Selected Outdoor Sculpture Projects:
"Ceremonial Conjecture," Morristown, NJ (in conjunction with Penny Kaplan)
"Sculpture 1980," Baltimore, MD, 1980
"Outgrowth," Battery Park, NY, 1979
"Hellgate Maza," Wards Island, NY, 1979
"Lost Path," Easthampton, NY, 1979
"No Man's Land," Kutztown, PA, 1975
